D0641264

ECONOMETRIC MODEL BUILDING

ECONOMETRIC MODEL BUILDING

—A Comparative Study of Simultaneous Equation Systems—

by

Young Sik Jang

ASSOCIATE PROFESSOR OF ECONOMICS
STATE UNIVERSITY OF NEW YORK

1973
YONSEI UNIVERSITY PRESS
Seoul, Korea

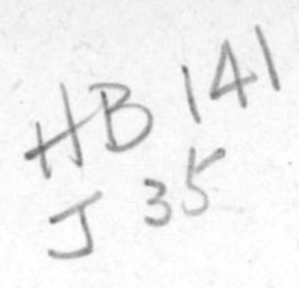

ECONOMETRIC MODEL BUILDING

First Printing: October 12, 1973
Second Printing: June 8, 1974

LIBRARY OF THE U.S. CONGRESS CATALOG CARD NO. 74–75518

Published by YONSEI UNIVERSITY PRESS
Seoul, Korea

PRINTED IN THE REPUBLIC OF KOREA

Preface

This book is the result of a number of years of research on the controversial problems and issues involved in econometric structural model building. These problems and issues were encountered in the process of actually preparing structural models, particularly aimed at economic forecasting, employing stationary, stochastic economic time series data. This is a quite natural consequence since model building is not an endeavor aimed at the construction of a unique, all-embracing theory.

The variety of plausible models is numerous for any given economic phenomenon. For this reason, the book focuses on the discussion between the two opposing approaches of structural model building: the Cowles Commission system of simultaneous equations, initiated by T. Haavelmo, and the Woldian Causal Chain (recursive) system of simultaneous equations, first intuitively employed by J. Tinbergen.

The discussion of the topic begins with an historical review and progresses ultimately to the current state of the controversy. No attempt has been made to render this book self-contained. However, certain portions may be easily utilized in courses of econometrics, especially when they have been preceded by an introductory course in econometrics. Such an introductory course should offer some insight into the problems of identification as well as some understanding of the Lundberg-Lindahl type of disequilibrium dynamic process and the Walras-Keynes type of equilibrium assumption.

The book should, however, be of particular interest to practicing economists who prepare ex-ante forecasts for decision making and planning in terms of structural models, as well as to academic economists and students who are interested in the theoretical questions involved in the field of econometric model building.

Finally, it is a pleasure to express my gratitude to those who have contributed directly or indirectly to the writing of this book. I would particularly like to thank Drs. Louis R. Salkever and Franklin V. Walker, who studied the entire manuscript and made many valuable criticisms and suggestions. Also, I am intellectually indebted to Dr. Herman O.A. Wold, for his many path-breaking research writings in monographs and articles on causal chain systems and time series analysis. I, of course, assume responsibility for all errors.

Part of this study was sponsored, through fellowships, by the State University of New York Research Foundation, Inc. and by the State University of New York at Albany Center.

Young Sik Jang

State University of New York
Plattsburgh, New York
November, 1973

CONTENTS

List of Tables

List of Illustrations

CHAPTER I

INTRODUCTION

CHAPTER I

INTRODUCTION

The inapplicability of controlled experimentation to economic phenomena creates an atmosphere of deep controversy for the econometrician, especially as he attempts the construction of dynamic, multirelated, structural models. His task is further complicated by the fact that model-building is not an endeavor aimed at the construction of a unique, all-embracing theory. The variety of plausible models is numerous for any given phenomenon and the econometrician therefore must scrutinize the various existing types of structural models. It is important that he comprehend the theoretical issues involved as well as establish future guidelines for the practical application of model-building.

The two most sophisticated, but opposing approaches to structural model-building, are the Cowles Commission system of simultaneous equations, initiated by Haavelmo,[1] and the Woldian recursive (causal chain) system of simultaneous equations, first employed by Tinbergen.[2] The Cowles or Haavelmo simultaneous equations system is called the "interdependent-system" (for brevity, hereafter the ID-system) in order

[1]Trygve Haavelmo, "The Statistical Implicatons of a System of Simultaneous Equations, " *Econometrica*, XI (January, 1943), 1–12 and his "The Probability Approach in Econometrics, " *Econometrica*, XII, Supplement (July, 1944), 118 pp.

[2]Jan Tinbergen, *Business Cycles in the United States of America, 1919–1932* (Geneva: League of Nations, 1939), 244 pp.

to distinguish it from the Woldian simultaneous causal chain equations system (hereafter, the CC-system). As a matter of current practice, the former has been employed usually as if it were the best approach, without giving any reasonable study to the latter; alternatively the single equation model has been applied without considering the whole network of structural relations.

The main purpose of this study therefore will be to compare the theoretical and operational rationale of the two systems in order to establish future guidance in the practical application of dynamic structural model-building. This comparison will be conducted in light of the systems' merits and demerits while at the same time, critically evaluating their fundamentals. Subsequently, an attempt will be made to demonstrate the unreasonableness of uncritical acceptance of one system while discrediting the other without a careful scrutiny of the theoretical and operational rationale of each. In addition, this study will clarify the true significance of the CC-system and will make the argument against the misinterpretation of the system by which the whole network of structural relations has been ignored. The basic view of this study will be oriented more toward a microeconomic foundation rather than a macroeconomic one.

A synthesis of the two approaches, however, will not be pursued in this paper. Such a synthesis would provide a basis for the indisputable applicability of the systems in every case. But this accomplishment is impossible, unless the two opposing philosophies of "causality" and "interdependency" could be synthesized. In addition, because modern econometric problems (such as autocorrelation, errors in variables, multicollinearity, etc.) raise analogous questions in the two systems, such problems will not be treated in this comparative study.[3]

THE PLAN OF THE STUDY

The divergent developments of the two systems will be reviewed briefly

---

[3]In other words, the following simple assumptions will not be relaxed throughout this study: (1) disturbance terms are normally and independently distributed stochastic variables with zero means and constant variances; (2) disturbance terms are uncorrelated with exogenous variables for all observation; and (3) all variables are observed without errors of measurement.

For a formal and precise description of these assumptions, see Chapter III, (A).

in Chapter II. Because these divergences are rooted in the conventional, static economic "equilibrium" approach and the "disequilibrium" processes, these methods will be defined technically within the boundaries of this comparative study.

In Chapter III "the least squares bias" in the parameter estimation will be evaluated through an ID-model to introduce the Cowles ID-system through a technical version. It will include theoretical as well as operational implications for the systems. From this discussion, several theoretically and operationally inherent dilemmas in the ID-system will be presented in detail in order to argue the uncritical acceptance of the ID-approach for structural model-building.

In Chapter IV the Woldian CC-system will be developed in depth as a legitimate alternative approach to the ID-system. Here a rationalization for the assumption of the CC-system will be rigorously developed through this author's two corollaries to the Wold Proximity Theorem. In addition, a much misunderstood meaning and implication of the term "causality" in the CC-system will be discussed in order to introduce a theoretical rationale and operational implication for the CC-system.

In contrast, Chapter V will recognize the merits of the two opposing systems. The Woldian attempts will be presented as a compromise version of the ID- and CC-systems. This third system will be called a Causalized-interdependent system, under which Bicausal-chain and Circular-chain systems will be classified as subsystems. Accordingly, economic theory will be deemphasized in order to stress the various possible compromise models in terms of the Gauss-Markoff processes.

In Chapter VI the Tin-Can Industry will be used as a case study of the two opposing systems and of the compromise system. For the purposes of this study, these models will be rigidly constructed in order to derive models as similar as possible, using the same time-series data. This construction will permit a more legitimate comparison of the merits and demerits of each system as well as a comparison of the different estimates yielded from these similar models. As was mentioned, the well-known time-series problem will not be treated as it would be treated in actual industrial study.

Finally, Chapter VII will draw conclusions from the data developed in the study, and some interesting fields for further investigation will be suggested.

CHAPTER II

A REVIEW AND PRELIMINARY DISCUSSION

CHAPTER II

A REVIEW AND PRELIMINARY DISCUSSION

The different approaches of the Interdependent (ID) and Causal-Chain (CC) systems are inherited from earlier attempts at empirical analysis employing the single equation models presented by such pioneers as Moore,[1] Working,[2] Schultz,[3] and others. The arguments in support of the two approaches are related to the "choice-of-regression" arguments of the 1920's and 1930's which arose during the transition from deterministic (mathematical) to stochastic models.[4] Actually, no controversy arose regarding the method of solution, as long as the model was specified as deterministic. But how these earlier arguments led to an intensive search

[1]Henry L. Moore, "Empirical Laws of Demand and Supply and the Flexibility of Prices," *Political Science Quarterly,* XXXIV (December, 1919), 546–67; and "A Moving Equilibrium of Demand and Supply," *Quarterly Journal of Economics,* XLI (May, 1925), 357–71.

[2]Elmer J. Working, "What Do Statistical 'Demand Curves' Show?," *Quarterly Journal of Economics,* LXI (February, 1927), 212–35.

[3]Henry Schultz, *The Meaning of Statistical Demand Curves* ed. by E. Altschul, (University of Chicago, February, 1930), 118pp. (Mimeographed).

[4]For a review of the thinking on this matter by applied economists up to the 1930s, see Henry Schultz, *The Theory and Measurement of Demand*; Chicago: University of Chicago Press, 1938), 817pp. Schultz's discussion of the general issue is in *ibid.*, particularly pp. 146–49.

for novel approaches can be understood, for example, by Frisch's *Confluence Analysis*.[5] In this analysis, Frisch denounced the uncritical use of the least-squares method and presented alternative regression methods.

On the eve of these arguments in 1943, Haavelmo formally denounced the direct application of the least-squares method to each of the behavioral relations, separately, without taking into consideration a whole network of relationships which apparently occur in the economic structure where the relations to be estimated originate.[6] His summary condemnation of the classical single-equation approach was based upon the economic model in which a mutual interdependency among the economic variables was assumed as a normal property.

In operational terms, "it is impossible to derive statistically the demand functions from market data without specifications of the supply functions involved" and without specifications of the equilibrium assumption of the demand and supply equations.[7] Because there are usually two or more endogenous variables in each relation, it is impossible to specify which endogenous variable is the dependent one. Second, no matter which one is selected, the remaining endogenous variable(s) can be correlated with the disturbance term in that relation. Third, the likelihood of determining the dependent endogenous variable is improbable because the endogenous variables are always mutually determined by each other in terms of the joint probability law. Thus the single-equation approach yields biased estimates of the structural parameters for a finite sample size, but the estimates are also inconsistent; that is, a bias persists even for infinitely large samples.

Related to the foundation of modern econometric analysis briefly

---

[5]Ragnar Frisch, *Statistical Confluence Analysis by Means of Complete Regression Systems* (Oslo: University Institute of Economics, 1934), p. 67.

Frisch advocates the use of diagonal regression as a compromise solution. Later, he and Haavelmo apply the diagonal regression method to family budget data to calculate income elasticity for milk in Norway. See Ragnar Frisch and Trygve Haavelmo, "The Demand for Milk in Norway," *Statsokonomisk Tidsskrift*, LII (1938), 47 as quoted in Herman Wold, "A Synthesis of Pure Demand Analysis," *Skandinavisk Aktuarietidskrift*, XXVII (1944), 112.

[6]Trygve Haavelmo, "The Statistical Implications of a System of Simultaneous Equations, " *Econometrica*, XI (January, 1943), 1–12.

[7]M. A. Girshick and Trygve Haavelmo, "Statistical Analysis of the Demand for Food: Examples of Simultaneous Estimation of Structural Equations, " *Econometrica*, XV (April, 1947), especially p. 83. The articles is reprinted with revision in Wm. C. Hood and Tjalling C. Koopmans (eds.), *Studies in Econometric Method,* Cowles Commission for Research in Economics, Monograph No. 14 (New York: John Wiley & Sons, 1953), pp. 92–111.

outlined above, is a study initiated by Tinbergen[8] who in 1939, intuitively evolved structural models through the use of simultaneous equations. In contrast to Haavelmo's argument, Tinbergen's approach is conducted by a "consecutive" analysis (simply known as causal-chain or recursive analysis) under a recursivity assumption; consequently, each structural equation is estimated by the least-squares method. Later, Wold rationalized Tinbergen's intuitive approach by a generalization of Yule's autoregressive process in order to establish simultaneous equations as the structural form, and by Kolmogorove's fundamental theorem for predictive inference.[9]

Wold's original theme is based upon the "disequilibrium" hypothesis as a normal property in a structural model. Wold's theme is thus contrary to Haavelmo's approach which focuses on the equilibrium assumption and rules out the possibility of disequilibrium in any structural model. In addition, Wold's theme basically defends the soundness of the least-squares method as an estimator of structural coefficients, and initiates "a method of using stochastic difference equations in econometric research," based upon the ideas of "process analysis" or "dynamic economics."[10] Furthermore according to the Bentzel and Wold Theorem,[11] if recursivity is implemented in a simultaneous equations model, assuming the conventional normality and independency of the disturbance terms, then the least-squares regression is identical to the full-information maximum likelihood method. Consequently, the classical "single-equation" approach can provide unbiased estimation of parameters, if a recursivity or causality is assumed as a normal property of a system of simultaneous equations; although in general, the approach is inadequate in estimating structural parameters if a mutual interdependency or simultaneity among the economic variables is inherent in the system. Once the stochastic structure

---

[8]Jan Tinbergen, *Business Cycles in the United States of America 1919–32* (Geneva: League of Nations, 1939); and his "Econometric Business Cycle Research," *Review of Economic Studies,* VII (1940), 73–90, which is reprinted in *Readings in Business Cycle Theory* (ed. Howard S. Ellis, Homewood, Illinois: Richard D. Irwin, 1944), pp. 61–86.

[9]For details, see Chapter IV.

[10]See Gerhard Tintner, *Econometrics* (New York: John Wiley & Sons, 1952), p. 275; R. Bentzel and H. Wold, "On Statistical Demand Analysis from the Viewpoint of Simultaneous Equations," *Skandinavisk Aktuarietidskrift,* XXIX (1946), 95–114; and H. Wold, "Statistical Estimation of Economic Relationships," *Econometrica,* XVII (1949), supplement, 1–22.

[11]Bentzel and Wold, *ibid.,* p. 106.

For a proof of the theorem, see an example, C. E. V. Leser, *Econometric Techniques and Problems,* Griffin's Statistical Monographs & Courses, No. 21, ed. by M. G. Kendall: (New York: Hafner Publishing Co., 1966), pp. 44–45 and E. Malinvaud, *Statistical Methods of Econometrics* (Chicago: Rand McNally & Co., 1966), pp. 540–43.

of a model is specified, however, parameter estimation becomes a purely technical problem and therefore, in principle, non-controversial.

In short, the ID-system is characterized distinctively by its formal property of mutual interdependency among economic variables—this is indicated by an assumption of *equilibrium* relations in the system; whereas, the related approach of Wold adopts causality among the variables from an assumption of *disequilibrium* in the system. These conflicting but fundamental arguments regarding assumptions arose after Haavelmo's criticism of the least-squares method in 1943. In opposition, Wold attacked the Haavelmo School as a static approach derived from the assumption of instantaneous equilibria. While defending the least-squares approach, Wold argued against the formal property of mutual interdependency among all economic behaving units which, at least within certain time periods, he believed to be autonomous.

So far "disequilibrium" and "equilibrium" assumptions have been mentioned as respectively upholding causality and interdependency in structural model-building. Before proceeding with further discussion, it would be worthwhile to mention the "disequilibrium" approach of the Stockholm School,[12] which introduces causality to the process of dynamic structural model-building. To explain this approach, the equilibrium method is utilized because it is well-known and can serve as a reference point for the "disequilibrium" approach employed in this paper.

According to Lindahl's synthesis of the Stockholm School's view,[13] every economic behaving unit (e.g., producer, government, etc.) in reality develops a plan (formal or informal) before acting. Its conditioned or unconditioned plan is based upon expectations which, in turn, are more or less conditioned by the unit's productive capacity, contracts, *a priori* commitments, etc. These expectations or anticipations of future events may not be caused by the past, but this fact does not imply that a unit should not allow its past experiences to assist in the decision-making process.

After completing this latter process, the unit evaluates it in light of ex-post realization. In this evaluation the discrepancy or disequilibrium is generally found between the expectation and realization. This discrepancy causes "disappointment" or "surprised realization" for the unit evaluators

[12]For example, see Erik Lundberg, *Studies in the Theory of Economic Expansion* Stockholm, 1939, Reprints of Economic Classics (New York: Augustus M. Kelley, Bookseller, 1964), especially pp. 181–242.

[13]Erik Lindahl, *Studies in the Theory of Money and Capital* (London: Allen & Unwin, 1939), particularly pp. 36ff.

and subsequently plays a significant role in forming the next period's expectation and plan.[14]

Figure 1

An Illustration of the Disequilibrium Approach.

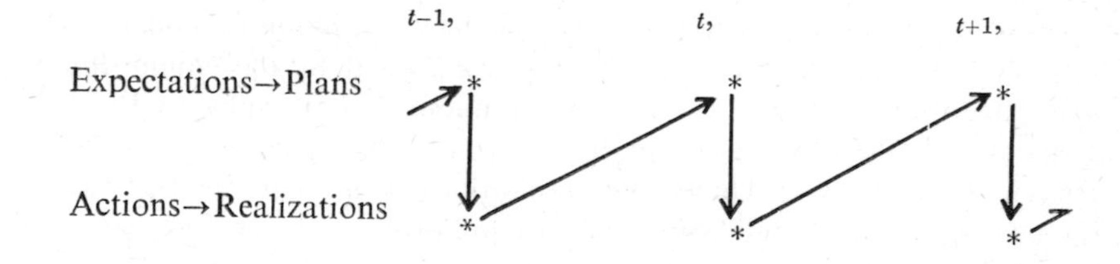

Figure 1 illustrates the process involved in the disequilibrium approach. The arrows show how the process is carried out during the time period and between the time periods. The sequential movement of "disequilibrium" appears as causal relationships or driving forces of the system in terms of a difference equation. For example, the conventional demand (or supply) curve is interpreted as conditioned plans. When a specific price is announced by a seller, the conditioned plans for buyers become unconditioned plans. Of course, plans may be "alterable" or "unalter-

Figure 2

Examples of Conditioned and Unconditioned Plans.

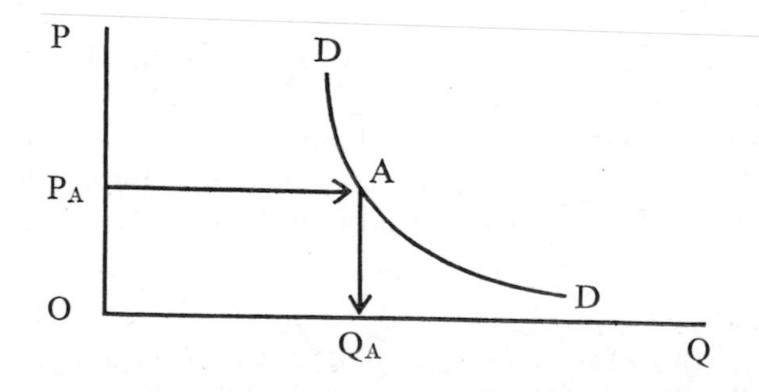

[14]This does not rule out the possibility of an equality between expectation and realization; see Bertil Ohlin, "Some Notes on the Stockholm Theory of Savings and Investment," *Economic Journal*, XLVII (March, 1937), 53–69; reprinted in *Readings in Business Cycle Theory* (Homewood, Illinois: Richard D. Irwin, 1951), pp. 87–130

able. "

Figure 2 shows the relationships between the conditioned and unconditioned plans. $\overline{DD}$ denotes the conditioned plans which later become unconditioned plans at point "Λ" . At a definite moment in time, disequilibrium creates temporary equilibrium.[15] The unidirectional arrows denote causality in the model. The further implication and meaning of the causality will be presented in detail in later chapters.

In reality, however, prices do not change continuously under the influence of demand and supply factors as posited by the equilibrium method; rather, price changes are discontinuous and are influenced by a series of disequilibria which, in turn, form a discontinuous series of temporary equilibria.[16] Under such conditions, it becomes evident that the two approaches, equilibrium and disequilibrium, can coexist together by supplementing each other. An example is the Keynesian static relationships which have been used in many "dynamic" studies in the post Keynesian era.[17]

Although the traditional approach from static to dynamic, is useful, especially for pedagogical sense, this approach is neither a necessary condition nor suitable in many cases. If the main purpose of economic theory is to explain the connections between certain given conditions and their corresponding developments, "economic theory should if possible be so framed as to be applicable to real conditions from the beginning, " contrary to the traditional approach.[18] In such a case it becomes necessary to demonstrate causal relations among the phenomena studied and to investigate the development from initial conditions to resulting developments.[19] The traditional approach fails to meet these challenges and loses its utility.

To paraphrase the above in operational terms concerning a market model, $S = D$ (where S = supply and D = demand) is a rigid static assumption from its inception, while a more flexible implication of $S \gtreqless D$ is better from its beginning both for open and closed market models. The plan to produce and to purchase is formed by different economic behaving units; consequently, in general, there is no warranty

---

[15]See John R. Hicks, *Value and Capital* (2d ed., Oxford: The Clarendon Press, 1946), pp. 115–27. The temporary equilibrium is based on Marshall's "short-period equilibrium."

[16]Lindahl, *Studies in the Theory of Money and Capital,* p. 60.

[17]For example, see Samuelson, "Dynamic Process Analysis" in *A Survey of Contemporary Economics* ed. by H. S. Ellis (Philadelphia: Blakiston, 1948), pp. 352–87.

[18]Lindahl, *Studies in the Theory of Money and Capital,* pp. 11–25.

[19]*Ibid.*

of the condition, $S = D$.[20] Practically, the discrepancy between S and D is a major condition for the next period's expectation, which, in turn, is a driving force in the market model. (As was implied formerly, the discrepancy in special cases includes that of non-discrepancy.)

In addition, static equilibrium conditions (special hypothesis) do not necessarily lead to interdependency. For example, in "the simple Keynesian model, $I =$ a constant, $S = f(Y)$, and $I = S$, S denoting saving. This static equilibrium model is recursive."[21]

Finally, although plans and actions of subunits (e.g., the production unit and sales unit of a firm) appear to be simultaneous or interdependent behavior, their interdependency arises from the inadequate conceptual division of economic behaving units. In reality these plans and actions "belong to the same behaving unit . . . and do not belong to the field of interest of economics."[22] Consequently, simultaneous behaviors of colluded duopolists can be conceived as the outcome of the same unit. It is much better therefore to justify an interdependency assumption of a model with an aggregation of ex-post data over a long period of time, and with a simplified version of the model for empirical studies, rather than a static equilibrium assumption as a condition for an unspecified dynamic system.[23]

In spite of these justifications of interdependency in the model, it can be argued that it is neither necessary nor appropriate in many cases to build an ID-model as an approximation before constructing a dynamic or CC-model. For instance, when the purpose of model-building is focused on a direction of movement or tendency of a variable, one can examine such movement direction through the "disequilibrium" approach, i.e., by implementing causality in a model. In this situation, these approaches can produce a better description of movements than can an ID-model.

Lindahl said:

"the scientific treatment . . . must . . . be based on a subdivision of the development into fairly short periods, it is of course impossible for the economist to follow it in detail from period to period. In spite of this, it

---

[20]Ohlin, "Some Notes on the Stockholm Theory of Savings and Investment," *Economic Journal*, XLVII (March, 1937), 53–69 and (June, 1937), 221–240.

[21]R. Bentzel and B. Hansen, "On Recursiveness and Interdependency in Economic Models," *Review of Economic Studies*, XXII (1954–55), 161.

[22]*Ibid.*, p. 159.

[23]Paul Samuelson said that a static equilibrium system can be conceived as the limiting case of a damped dynamic model; from his *Foundations of Economic Analysis* (Cambridge: Harvard University Press, 1947), pp. 262ff.

is quite feasible to give a picture of the course of events during a fairly long stretch of time. If by the analysis of certain selected typical periods, one can determine the directions of movement during these stretches, the character of the intervening periods may also be understood . . .
. . . it is impossible for the economist to give a complete analysis of a complicated course of development in one and the same exposition. He must usually be content to discuss the total developments from some special point of view . . . "[24]

At this point, having presented the comparative historical development of the ID- and CC-systems, which are antithetical to each other, and having described the essential differences of the equilibrium and disequilibrium approaches, this study will proceed to develop typical examples of each system. These illustrations will serve to demonstrate further the technical characteristics of each system and to rigorously define them for use in this study.

A. THE ID-SYSTEM

Let us postulate a simple ID-system of an agricultural crop market under competition, which consists of a linear supply relation and a linear demand relation, together with an equilibrium assumption, namely,

(1) $S_t = a_1P_t + b_1X_{1t} + u_{1t}$ (Supply Relation)

(2) $D_t = a_2P_t + b_2X_{2t} + u_{2t}$ (Demand Relation)

(3) $S_t = D_t = Q_t$ (Instantaneous Equilibrium)

(with $t = 1, 2, \ldots, T$).

To facilitate analysis, the variables are measured as deviations from their mean values. S_t is a quantity supplied during time period, t; D_t is a quantity demanded in t; P_t is a price of the crop in t. Q_t and P_t are endogenous variables to be explained by the system. X_{1t} is rainfall; X_{2t} is per capita income. X_{1t} and X_{2t} are assumed as exogenous variables, u_{1t} and u_{2t} are disturbance terms which are assumed normally and independently distributed, and uncorrelated with exogenous variables for all t. For simplicity, errors in variables are not considered. Symbolically, $E(u_{it}) = 0$

[24]Lindahl, *Studies in the Theory of Money and Capital,* p. 59.

$(i = 1, 2)$; $E(u_{it}, X_{it}) = 0$; $E(u_{it}, u_{it+k}) = \sigma^2$ when $k = 0$ or 0 when $k \neq 0$. $(k = 1, 2, \ldots; i = 1, 2)$.

In the above equation (1), a key point of the ID-system is examined. Even though P_{t-1} is substituted for P_t, as in a cobweb model which is usually claimed to be "dynamic," the system appears to be more static than dynamic. According to general scientific terminology, dynamic analysis involves the study of movements which are generated by a system of forces, and static analysis deals with special cases when movements

Arrow Scheme Specifications of Interdependency

Figure 3–A **Figure 3–B**

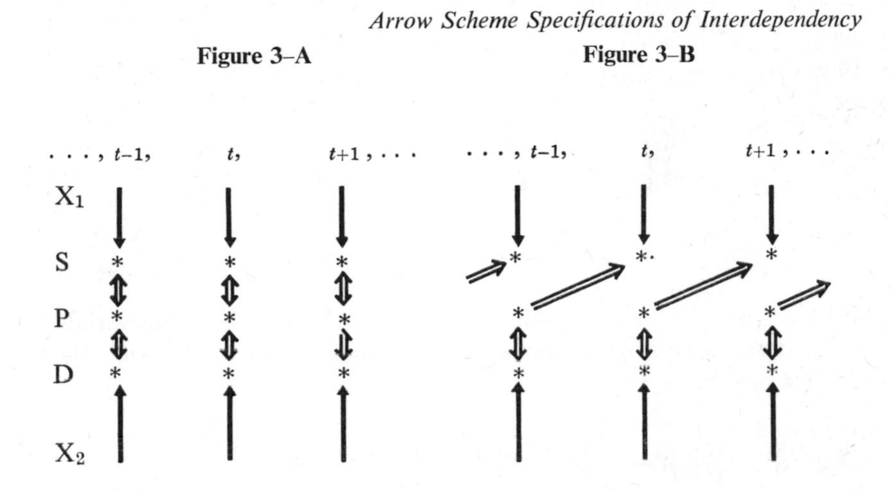

are in equilibrium. Therefore, the system in reality cannot be said to be dynamic due to its equilibrium, regardless of its inclusion of lagged variables.[25]

For the sake of comparative illustration, the famous arrow scheme explanation, including the case of substitution of P by P_{-1}, will be applied to the above model. In Figure 3-A, the main feature of interdependency within the ID-system is shown by the bi-directional double line arrows among the endogenous variables, S, P, and D. This case is a perfectly indecomposable variety of an interdependent model. In Figure 3-B, the bi-directional arrows disappear between P and S, when P_{-1} is substituted

---

[25]When P_t is substituted by P_{t-1} the model is a moving equilibrium model. According to Marc Nerlove, *Distributed Lags and Demand Analysis for Agricultural and Other Commodities,* U.S. Dept. of Agriculture Handbook No. 141 (Washington: U.S. Government Printing Office, 1958), p. 1, "in economics, a cause often produces its effect only after a lapse of time." This quotation will be considered in the CC-system below.

for P. This case is an imperfectly indecomposable variety of an interdependent model. In short, the existence of bi-directional arrows in the diagram, in general, indicates an interdependent model.

The structural equations for the ID-system can be rewritten in matrix form, using familiar matrix notation to provide a compact explanation of the system:

$$\text{(4a)} \quad \begin{bmatrix} 1 & 0 \\ 1 & 0 \end{bmatrix} \begin{bmatrix} S_t \\ D_t \end{bmatrix} = \begin{bmatrix} a_1 & 0 \\ 0 & a_2 \end{bmatrix} \begin{bmatrix} P_t \\ P_t \end{bmatrix} + \begin{bmatrix} b_1 & 0 \\ 0 & b_2 \end{bmatrix} \begin{bmatrix} X_{1t} \\ X_{2t} \end{bmatrix} + \begin{bmatrix} u_{1t} \\ u_{2t} \end{bmatrix}$$

$$S_t = D_t = Q_t$$

or

$$\text{(4b)} \quad Dy_t = C\bar{y}_t + BX_t + u_t$$

where

$$D = \begin{bmatrix} 1 & 0 \\ 1 & 0 \end{bmatrix}; \; y_t = \begin{bmatrix} Q_t \\ Q_t \end{bmatrix}; \; \bar{y}_t = \begin{bmatrix} P_t \\ P_t \end{bmatrix}; \; C = \begin{bmatrix} a_1 & 0 \\ 0 & a_2 \end{bmatrix}$$

$$B = \begin{bmatrix} b_1 & 0 \\ 0 & b_2 \end{bmatrix}; \; X_t = \begin{bmatrix} X_{1t} \\ X_{2t} \end{bmatrix}; \; u_t = \begin{bmatrix} u_{1t} \\ u_{2t} \end{bmatrix};$$

the "—" in $\bar{y}_t$ is used to distinguish the right-hand endogenous variables from the left-hand endogenous variables in the structural form. Then, (4) can be written as,

$$\text{(5a)} \quad \begin{bmatrix} 1 & -a_1 \\ 1 & -a_2 \end{bmatrix} \begin{bmatrix} Q_t \\ P_t \end{bmatrix} = \begin{bmatrix} b_1 & 0 \\ 0 & b_2 \end{bmatrix} \begin{bmatrix} X_{1t} \\ X_{2t} \end{bmatrix} + \begin{bmatrix} u_{1t} \\ u_{2t} \end{bmatrix}$$

or

$$\text{(5b)} \quad AY_t = BX_t + u_t$$

Where $AY_t = Dy_t - Cy_t$; and

$$Y_t = \begin{bmatrix} Q_t \\ P_t \end{bmatrix} \qquad A = \begin{bmatrix} 1 & -a_1 \\ 1 & -a_2 \end{bmatrix}$$

Technically, the ID-systems have the formal property of the block-form coefficient matrix for endogenous variables. The matrix is an indecomposible variety of interdependency in either perfect or imperfect form.

Therefore, the solution or the reduced form for endogenous variables, Q_t and P_t, is:

$$\text{(6a)} \quad \begin{bmatrix} Q_t \\ P_t \end{bmatrix} = (a_1 - a_2)^{-1} \begin{bmatrix} -b_1a_2X_{1t} + a_1b_2X_{2t} - a_1u_{2t} - a_2u_{1t} \\ -b_1X_{1t} + b_2X_{2t} + u_{2t} - u_{1t} \end{bmatrix}$$

or

$$\text{(6b)} \quad Y_t = A^{-1}BX_t + A^{-1}u_t$$

$= MX_t + w_t$

where $A^{-1}B = M$; $A^{-1}u_t = w_t$

In (4b), the matrix D is not the identity matrix and C is a block form matrix; A in (5b) is a block form matrix. Accordingly, it is self-explanatory why the whole network of values of parameters changes if any one of its values changes, i.e., this is a formal property of the ID-system. In other words, two or more endogenous variables in the system mutually depend upon each other due to the joint probability law. Therefore, u_{1t} and u_{2t} cannot be treated as random variables for P_t or Q_t, respectively. Changes in either u_{1t} or u_{2t} cause shifts, with respect to time, in the level of both supply and demand curves. This point will be made clear when the coefficients of the exogenous variables, b_1 and b_2, are set at zero *a priori*, as was done by Haavelmo.[26] In this case, there is no way of differentiating between the supply and demand curves.

As we have seen, the autonomous nature of the system's behavioral relations, which arc the main building materials for models, naturally becomes non-autonomous due to the symmetry and uncontrolled reversibility derived from the technical method of arriving at the reduced form used for predictive inference. In other words, the ID-system's structural form is constructed according to economic theory in order to develop the reduced form for predictive inference. But this structural form, derived from economic theory, has only an auxiliary role in the derivation of the prediction equations, i.e., the reduced form of equations.[27]

B. THE CC-SYSTEM

A typical CC-system may be similar to the ID-system and is constructed as follows:

(1) $S_t = a_1P_{t-1} + b_1X_{1t} + u_{1t}$ (Supply Relation)

(2) $D_t = a_2P_t + b_2X_{2t} + u_{2t}$ (Demand Relation)

[26]"The Statistical Implications of a System of Simultaneous Equations."

[27]Haavelmo states that "for prediction purposes the original equations of the system have no practical significance, they play only the role of theoretical tools by which to derive the prediction equation." See Haavelmo, "The Statistical Implications of a System of Simultaneous Equations," p. 11.

(3) $P_t = P_{t-1} + g(D_t^* - S_t^*) + b_3X_{2t} + u_{3t}$ (Price Mechanism or Merchant's Behavior)

where "*" in (3) denotes *ex-ante* values and the rest of the notations are the same as in (A) above.

Operationally, $(S_t^* - D_t^*)$ is different from industry to industry. For the sake of simplicity, consider that $S_t^* = S_t$, assuming that producers' expectations are approximately correct, and that $D_t^* = D_{t-1}$, assuming that consumers' expectations or planned purchases are heavily ruled by the inertia effect or habit. Then (3) can be rewritten as $P_t = P_{t-1} + g(S_t - D_{t-1}) + X_{2t} + u_{3t}$. Of course, S_{t-1} might be substituted for S_t in a different industry. However $g(S_t - D_t)$, i.e., both denote the current period and should be avoided in order to make the CC-system.

A fundamental departure from the ID-system occurs in (3) which, in general, implies $S_t \gtreqless D_t$, because S_t and D_t are regulated by the different economic units, producers and consumers. The endogenous variables must be classified as explained (effect) and explanatory (cause) variables. The explanatory endogenous variables are assumed as uncorrelated with the residual terms in the probability limit, so as to make the CC-system. In symbols $E(u_{it}) = 0$; $E(u_{it}, X_{it}) = E(u_{it}, P_{t-1}) = 0$; $E(P_t, u_{2t}) = 0$; $E(D_t^*, u_{3t}) = E(S_t^*, u_{3t}) = 0$ with $i = 1, 2, 3$. This is based on the implication of Wold's proximity theorem. Because Wold's proximity theorem needs some detailed treatment as well as some clarification in order to apply directly to the CC-system, we will discuss the problem including our corollary to the theorem in Chapter IV.

The time lag in (1) is set by a "retarded reaction" assumption which is the crucial essence of the CC-system. That is, without the lag, the model is not a CC-system. The time lag is an "important step in the development toward a full-fledged dynamic model,"[28] and a CC-model cannot be constructed without making this dynamic assumption.

The merchants' behavior relation, price mechanism or market mechanism are built on an explicit specification, rather than on an implicit assumption as in the ID-system. This system explicitly recognizes that the producers and consumers are brought into the market by merchants. (Of course, a producer can play the merchant's role.) The merchant's role is analogous to a catalyzer in chemistry. For example, to produce H_20, hydrogen and oxygen must be brought together by the catalyst in an experiment. Although $2H_2 + 0_2 = 2H_20$, the *symbolic equation* of the

[28]Marc Nerlove, *Distributed Lags and Demand Analysis* (Agriculture Handbook No. 141, Washington, D.C.: Government Printing Office, 1958), p. 1.

experiment does not denote the catalyzer. The *operational design* of the experiment, however, should explicitly specify the catalyzer's role. Thus, the explicit specification for the system in (3) is a fundamental departure from the implicit assumption in the ID-system.[29] Furthermore, (3) may develop an equilibrium price faster than the implicit price relation of the ID-system, depending upon the values of g.[30]

Finally, the system of equations, (1), (2), (3), should be logically specified recursively, link-by-link, from one period to the next in a chain of explicit specifications for the model, resulting in an arrow scheme diagram:

Figure 4.
The Arrow Scheme of the CC-System

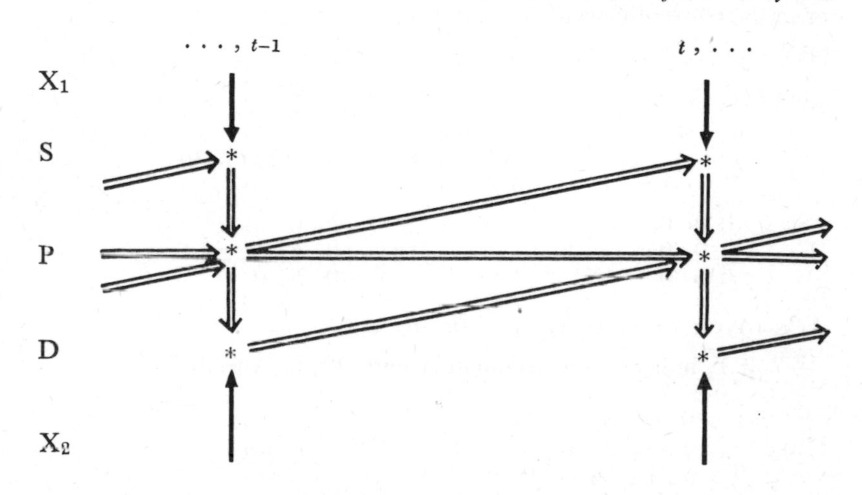

The double-line arrows indicate causal influences among the current and lagged endogenous variables, S, P and D; the single-line arrows indicate the influence of exogenous variables, X_1, X_2. Specifically, S_t is causally explained by P_{t-1} and X_{1t}; P_t, by P_{t-1} as well as the excess demand, $(S_t - D_{t-1})$ and X_{2t}; and D_t, by P_t and X_{2t}. As can be seen, the arrows

[29]As was shown, in the ID-system, a price relation is derived as an inverse function of the quantity in terms of the reduced form.

[30]g means the size or the speed of the price and adjustments; $g(s\text{-}d)$ links up the price movements with changes in the merchant's stock. The first work in this field was done by G. C. Evans, *The Mathematical Introduction to Economics* (New York: McGraw-Hill Co., 1930) particularly see pp. 47ff. Several models of this type of relation are analyzed by Paul A. Samuelson in "The Stability of Equilibrium: Comparative Statics and Dynamics, " *Foundations of Economic Analysis* (Cambridge: Harvard University Press, 1947), pp. 257–76. However, empirical tests in this direction are very rare.

flow only uni-directionally. This one-way flow of causation is the crucial assumption, which arises from the subject matter theory of the Woldian CC-system.

In line with the arrow scheme, the system must be respccified in accordance with the causal order in Figure 4. Then, the preliminary specifications of the causal order, (1), (2), (3), $(S_t\ D_t\ P_t)$ of the model are respecified as (1), (3), (2), $(S_t\ P_t\ D_t)$.

The system, (1), (3), (2), can be rewritten in matrix form as follows:

$$\text{(4a)}\quad \begin{bmatrix} 1 & 0 & 0 \\ 0 & 1 & 0 \\ 0 & 0 & 1 \end{bmatrix} \begin{bmatrix} S_t \\ P_t \\ D_t \end{bmatrix} = \begin{bmatrix} 0 & 0 & 0 \\ -g & 0 & 0 \\ 0 & a_2 & 0 \end{bmatrix} \begin{bmatrix} S_t \\ P_t \\ D_t \end{bmatrix} + \begin{bmatrix} b_1 & 0 & a_1 & 0 \\ 0 & b_3 & 1 & g \\ 0 & b_2 & 0 & 0 \end{bmatrix} \begin{bmatrix} X_{1t} \\ X_{2t} \\ P_{t-1} \\ D_{t-1} \end{bmatrix} + \begin{bmatrix} u_{1t} \\ u_{3t} \\ u_{2t} \end{bmatrix}$$

or in the conventional matrix notation:

$$\text{(4b)}\quad DY_t = IY_t = A\bar{Y}_t + BX_t + u_t$$

where

$$D = I = \begin{bmatrix} 1 & 0 & 0 \\ 0 & 1 & 0 \\ 0 & 0 & 1 \end{bmatrix};\quad Y_t = \bar{Y}_t = (S_t\ P_t\ D_t)$$

$$A = \begin{bmatrix} 0 & 0 & 0 \\ -g & 0 & 0 \\ 0 & a_2 & 0 \end{bmatrix};\qquad B = \begin{bmatrix} b_1 & 0 & a_1 & 0 \\ 0 & b_3 & 1 & g \\ 0 & b_2 & 0 & 0 \end{bmatrix}$$

$X_t = (X_{1t}\ X_{2t}\ P_{t-1}\ D_{t-1})$; $u_t = (u_{1t}\ u_{2t}\ u_{3t})$.

"—" in $\bar{Y}_t$ indicates the explanatory endogenous variables.

$$\text{(5a)}\quad \begin{bmatrix} 1 & 0 & 0 \\ g & 1 & 0 \\ 0 & -a_2 & 1 \end{bmatrix} \begin{bmatrix} S_t \\ P_t \\ D_t \end{bmatrix} = \begin{bmatrix} b_1 & 0 & a_1 & 0 \\ 0 & b_3 & 1 & g \\ 0 & b_2 & 0 & 0 \end{bmatrix} \begin{bmatrix} X_{1t} \\ X_{2t} \\ P_{t-1} \\ D_{t-1} \end{bmatrix} + \begin{bmatrix} u_{1t} \\ u_{2t} \\ u_{3t} \end{bmatrix}$$

or

$$\text{(5b)}\quad (I - A)\quad Y_t = BX_t + u_t$$

where

$$(I - A) = \begin{bmatrix} 1 & 0 & 0 \\ g & 1 & 0 \\ 0 & -a_2 & 1 \end{bmatrix}$$

Then, the reduced form of the system becomes:

$$\text{(6a)}\quad \begin{bmatrix} S_t \\ P_t \\ D_t \end{bmatrix} = \begin{bmatrix} a_1P_{t-1} + b_1X_{1t} + u_{1t} \\ -b_1gX_{1t} + b_3X_{2t} - (a_1g - 1)P_{t-1} + gD_{t-1} - gu_{1t} + u_{3t} \\ -b_1a_2gX_{1t} + (b_2 + a_2b_3)X_{2t} - (a_1a_2g - a_2)P_{t-1} \\ \quad + a_2gD_{t-1} + (a_2u_{3t} - a_2gu_{1t} + u_{2t}) \end{bmatrix}$$

or in the conventional matrix notation:

$$(6b) \quad Y = (I - A)^{-1}BX_t + (I - A)^{-1}u_t$$
$$= MX_t + w_t$$

where $(I - A)^{-1}B = M$ and $(I - A)^{-1} u_t = w_t$.

Thus in the above CC-system, the matrix $D = I$ (identity matrix); whereas in the ID-system, $D \neq I$.

The first step in arranging recursively the CC-system of equations specifies a chain of iterative substitutions of one equation after another in accordance with a specified order of causation. This flow process will produce the reduced form of the CC-system.[31] The square matrix A is a subdiagonal matrix which is termed "recursive" by Wold. $(I\text{-}A)^{-1}$ is a triangular matrix; variance-covariance matrix of u_t is diagonal.

Speaking operationally in probability terms, the expected values of S_t in (1) are substituted for S_t in (3) and then expected values of P_t in (3) are substituted for P_t in (2) in order to derive the reduced form of the CC-system. This process involves the operation of a chain of iterative substitutions, one-by-one, in accordance with the specification of the flow of causation. Although the parameters of the reduced form of the CC-system can be transformed into the parameter space of the structural form, this transformation is not always recommended because of the problem of identification and the risk of multicollinearity. The operation implies that the transformation of the structural parameters can be performed for a prediction of the endogenous variables, after a direct application of the least-squares operation if performed on the structural form.

Thus, the CC-system has the formal property of a subdiagonal matrix of explanatory endogenous variables which allow the variables to relate recursively one-by-one and equation-to-equation. This maintains the hypothesis of autonomy for any single behaving economic unit in reduced form, as it does in structural form, at least during the time period of execution of the behaving unit's plans. Thus, the structural form plays a major role in the Woldian system, contrary to the ID-system.

In other words, by the asymmetry and irreversibility property of the CC-system, any autonomous economic behaving unit may modify or

[31]Despite the definition of the "reduced form" by the ID-school, e.g., Carl F. Christ, *Econometric Models and Methods* (New York: John Wiley & Sons, 1966), p. 21, as "the set of non-autonomous derived equations, containing one endogenous variable, " the equation (6) in the ID-system as well as (6) in the CC-system are the reduced forms.

If any form of simultaneous equations is transferred so as to have only one endogenous variable in each equation, the set of transformed equations is the reduced form. Therefore, autonomy of nonautonomy of the derived relation is irrelevent in defining the reduced form.

alter its own behavior pattern without affecting the behavior pattern of other autonomous units at least during the time period of the execution of their plans. This assumption is based on the Stockholm School's period analysis or disequilibrium method, as previously described.

As a summary of the above description and example of the two typical systems, simplified definitions of the ID- and CC-systems are presented for use in future chapters.[32]

Although no standard definitions exist, *the ID-systems* may be defined as a system of stochastic, simultaneous equations which are specified to contain a matrix of the coefficients of endogenous variables in indecomposable block form. This form is due to equilibria assumptions and the aggregation of data, so that the autonomy of each behaving economic unit is not maintained in the reduced form. This result serves explicitly to explain and to predict the current endogenous variables in terms of the predetermined variables.

The CC-system may be defined as a system of stochastic simultaneous equations which are specified to include a matrix of the coefficients of endogenous variables in decomposable triangular form. This form is due to the disequilibria hypothesis and the subject-matter information, so that the autonomy of each behaving economic unit is maintained in the reduced form as well as in the structural form. These results serve explicitly to explain and to predict the behavior relations, in terms of explanatory variables, which are specified to maintain the covariance matrix of disturbance terms as diagonal.

According to the conceptual mathematical definitions of the two systems, the crucial differences occur due to the block form of the matrix in the ID-system. Here the block form imposes the property of mutual interdependency, while the triangular form of the matrix in the CC-system recursively explains the flow of causation. In addition, once the stochastic structure of a model is specified, parameter estimation becomes a problem which is purely technical and therefore, in principle, non-controversial. For the ID-system, the parameters of the reduced form are estimated and

[32]Definitions are rarely as informative as they claim to be; they often remain vague and their usefulness is limited. In fact they may be positively harmful, particularly if they are used as a pseudo-scientific justification for the convenient practice of considering evidence for or against particular conclusions—and remain outside the "proper" scope of the definition within a certain discipline. Even more harmful is the practice of using such definitions as instruments to channel research into only one direction or, consciously or unconsciously, to suppress evidence altogether.

For this reason the attempted definitions of the ID- and CC-systems acquire their full meaning and precision only as our acquaintance with the problems under study expands.

transformed back to the parameter space of the structural form. For the CC-system the least-squares regression method can be applied directly to each behavioral equation or can be applied to the reduced form of the CC-system, depending upon the purpose of the model-building.

CHAPTER III

THE INTERDEPENDENT SYSTEMS

CHAPTER III

THE INTERDEPENDENT SYSTEMS

It was a path-breaking achievement of the first magnitude for Haavelmo to show that reduced form equations must be employed to derive consistent and reversible estimates of structural relations between jointly dependent or endogenous variables. Accepting this interdependent system (ID-system) as an all-purpose econometric structural model, the Cowles Commission (now Foundation) researchers thoroughly explored various prominent estimation techniques. Their efforts proved that much of economic theory could be cast as a system of interdependent relations. As a result, there was no doubt that the ID-system, including its explicit incorporation of residual terms, would become the cornerstone of modern econometric analysis.

However, the ID-approach has not been a panacea for structural model-building and has many inherent problems or dilemmas. It is the central task of this chapter to present these dilemmas to lend some impetus toward an increased interest in alternative causal chain systems. In order to develop this main theme logically, historical arguments by Haavelmo in initiating his ID-system are presented below. His generalized version of the mechanical implication of the ID-system is presented in section (A) followed by a discussion of the dilemmas of the system in section (B).

As was discussed in the preceding chapter, the essential built-in mechanism which underlies interdependency in a model is the equilibrium assumption. This property of interdependency is an outcome of the Walras-Keynesian type of static equilibrium economic theory, which is supported by mathematical proof in a closed system. The static equilibrium theory is adopted by the joint probability law as a foundation for parameter estimation. On the other hand, if one were to accept instantaneous equilibrium or moving equilibrium, it would be impossible to select, subjectively, cause and effect variables among the economic variables in a model. For example, a demand relation in a simple supply and demand market model cannot be estimated satisfactorily by the least-squares single equations method, mainly due to the difficulty of deciding subjectively whether the quantity demanded or the price is the effect variable. Rather, each parameter in the relation must be estimated in terms of the model as a whole, by applying the joint probability law. Otherwise, the estimates would be biased for a finite sampling and also be inconsistent, i.e., "the least-squares bias."

"The least-squares bias" in parameter estimation will be illustrated by an example from Haavelmo.[1] In this example, the least-squares single equation method is applied directly to the interdependent nature of economic variables in a relation. In a theoretically simple relation dealing with two jointly dependent variables, Q and P are measured as deviations from their mean values, namely:

$$Q_t = aP_t + u_t \tag{1}$$

$$P_t = bQ_t + v_t \tag{2}$$

$$t = 1,2,\ldots,T$$

where variables u and v are "latent" or disturbance terms, which are assumed to be normally and independently distributed with a zero mean and constant variances equal to $\delta^2{}_u$ and $\delta^2{}_v$, respectively.[2] A characteristic feature of the Haavelmo approach, however, asserts that the a priori assumption refers to u and v, not Q and P. As the simplest case, Haavelmo assumes that u and v are uncorrelated, $r(u_t v_t) = 0$. That is, $\text{cov}(u_t v_t) = \text{Plim}\ (1/T)\ (u_t v_t) = 0$, where cov denotes covariance and Plim is the probability limit.

The parameters a and b cannot, in general, be estimated from (1) and (2) *sériatim* without yielding biases in its estimates. P and u are not uncorrelated in the probability limit, for it is evident that u affects Q through (1) and that Q in turn affects P through (2). To bring out the explicit

---

[1]Trygve Haavelmo, "The Statistical Implications of a System of Simultaneous Equations," *Econometrica*, XI (January, 1943), 1–12.

[2]See section (A) below for a complete treatment of specification.

dependence of P and Q, the reduced form would be formed as functions of u and v, namely:

$$Q_t = (u_t + av_t)/(1 - ab) \tag{3}$$

$$P_t = (bu_t + v_t)/(1 - ab) \tag{4}$$

so that

$$\begin{aligned}\text{Plim } (1/T)\, P_t u_t &= \text{cov } (P_t u_t) \\ &= (1 - ab)^{-1}[b \text{ var}(u_t) + \text{cov}(u_t v_t)] \\ &\neq 0 \text{ in general,}\end{aligned}$$

where var stands for variance.

In the structural form, (1) and (2), the parameters, a, b, $\delta^2{}_u$, and $\delta^2{}_v$ are unknown. From the reduced form, (3) and (4), it appears that only three parameters, $E(P^2)$, $E(Q^2)$, and $E(PQ)$, can be estimated. Therefore, it is impossible to estimate any parameters in the structural form.

The problem of identification is seen by presenting the statistically equivalent form of structural equations, obtained by adding (1) to (2):

$$\begin{aligned}Q &= -(1 - a)/(1 - b)P + (u + v)/(1 - b) \\ &= eP + w\end{aligned} \tag{5}$$

where
$$\begin{aligned}e &= -(1 - a)/(1 - b) \\ w &= (u + v)/(1 - b)\end{aligned}$$

$$\begin{aligned}P &= (1 + b)/(1 + a)Q + (-u + v)/(1 + a) \\ &= fP + w''\end{aligned} \tag{6}$$

where
$$\begin{aligned}f &= (1 + b)/(1 + a) \\ w'' &= (-u + v)/(1 + a)\end{aligned}$$

w and w'' are also normally and independently distributed.

Therefore, $e \neq a$ and $f \neq b$; and the variance of w and w'' ($\delta^2{}_w$ and $\delta^2{}_{w''}$) are different from the variance of u and v ($\delta^2{}_u$ and $\delta^2{}_v$), respectively. Nevertheless, (5) and (6) are consistent with observations and there is no way to be sure that an estimate supposedly of e.g., a, is not in fact an estimate of e. If $\delta^2{}_u = \delta^2{}_v$, the four unknown parameters (a, b, $\delta^2{}_u$, and $\delta^2{}_v$) are actually the same number as the three parameters which, in turn, are the same number as the unknown parameters in the reduced form, (3) and (4). Therefore, the parameters of (1) and (2) can uniquely be determined. In spite of these conditions, the structural form does not offer any advantage over the reduced form.

The usual interpretation of the reduced form is that there is no causal relation between P and Q, only a stochastic relation due to their common dependence on the primary variables, u and v. That is, (1) and (2) are shifted by u and v.

Another simple simultaneous equations model—here as a system of difference equations—shows another problem of statistical inference of the ID-system: the single equation least-squares method yields biased estimates of the parameters of the model.

Consider the structural form:

$$C_t = a + bY_t + u_{1t} \tag{7}$$

$$I_t = k(C_t - C_{t-1}) + u_{2t} \tag{8}$$

$$Y_t = C_t + I_t \tag{9}$$

C is consumption per year; Y is total income; I is investment; a, b, and k are coefficients; the residual u_{1t} and u_{2t} are assumed to be independently and normally distributed with a zero mean and a common variance.

The reduced form is:

$$C_t + m_{11}C_{t-1} + m_1 = w_{1t} \tag{10}$$

$$I_t + m_{21}C_{t-1} + m_2 = w_{2t} \tag{11}$$

Where the coefficients of the reduced form, m_{11}, m_{21}, m_1, and m_2 and variance-covariance, δw_{11}, δw_{22}, and δw_{12} can be expressed in terms of the five parameters of the structural form:

$$m_{11} = (bk)/(1 - b - bk) \qquad m_1 = (-a)/(1 - b - bk) \tag{12}$$

$$m_{21} = (k - bk)/(1 - b - bk) \qquad m_2 = (-bk)/(1 - b - bk)$$

$$\delta w_{11} = (\delta^2{}_{u_1} + b^2\delta^2{}_{u_2})/(1 - b - bk)^2 \tag{13}$$

$$\delta w_{12} = (k\delta^2{}_{u_1} + b(1 - b)\delta^2{}_{u_2})/(1 - b - bk)^2$$

$$\delta w_{22} = [k^2\delta^2{}_{u_1} + (1 - b)^2\delta^2{}_{u_2}]/(1 - b - bk)^2$$

When the single equation least-squares method is applied to the structural form, (7) and (8), separately, the condition:

$$E(C_t/Y_t) = a + bY_t \tag{14}$$

$$E[I_t/(C_t - C_{t-1})] = k(C_t - C_{t-1}) \tag{15}$$

should be satisfied. The above condition, however, implies that $E(Y_tu_{1t}) = E(C_t - C_{t-1})\, u_{2t} = 0$. This imposes a restriction upon the joint distribution of u_{1t} and u_{2t}. If the joint probability law of u_{1t} and u_{2t} is expressed as Prob($u_{1t}\ u_{2t}$) and the probability distribution of C_t and I_t, for a given C_{t-1}, is written as Prob(C_tI_t), transformations of (7) and (8) give at once

$$(16) \qquad \text{Prob}\,(C_t I_t) = (1 - b - bk)\ \text{prob}\,(u_{1t} u_{2t})$$
$$= /\det A/\text{Prob}\,(u_{1t} u_{2t})$$

where det A = the determinant of coefficients of endogenous

variables in (7) – (9), i.e., $\begin{bmatrix} b & 1 & 0 \\ 0 & k & 1 \\ 1 & -1 & -1 \end{bmatrix}$

$$u_{1t} = C_t - a - bY_t = C_t - a - b(C_t + I_t)$$

$$u_{2t} = I_t - k(C_t - C_{t-1})$$

The restriction (14) – (15) on one joint probability distribution is also a restriction on other distributions. Moreover, although (14) and (15) imply $E(u_{1t}) = 0 = E(u_{2t})$, the latter is not nceessarily the condition of the former.

A. MECHANICAL IMPLICATIONS OF THE STRUCTURAL FORM AND THE REDUCED FORM

At this point, let us assume economic theories that have the following sets of a linear model containing g- structural relations. The model can be written in matrix form as

$$(17) \qquad AY_t + BZ_t = U_t$$
$$t = 1,2,\ldots,T$$

where

A = a (gxg) nonsingular matrix of coefficients of Y_t

Y_t = a g-order column vector of endogenous variables

B_t = a (gxk) matrix of coefficients of Z_t

Z_t = a k-order column vector of predetermined variables[3]

[3]Technically, predetermined variables denote the lagged or unlagged exogenous variables and the lagged endogenous variables. Endogenous variables or jointly determined variables are the variables which are actually determined by the system of structural equations which we are investigating in the current observation t.

U_t = *a* g-order column vector of the disturbance terms.

The structural disturbances are assumed to be generated by a stationary multivariate stochastic process[4] with,

$$E(U_t) = 0. \tag{18}$$

In words, each disturbance vector has a zero expectation:

$$E(U_{it}U_{jt+\delta}) = V \quad \text{when } \delta = 0 \tag{19}$$
$$= 0 \quad \text{when } \delta \neq 0$$

where V is (gxg) non-negative definite matrix. The contemporaneous covariance matrix of the disturbances in the different eqations is the same for all t and the disturbance vector is temporarily in a diagonal matrix; all covariances between disturbances in equations are zero. All lagged covariances are assumed zero. In general, these assumptions imply that the variances and covariances of the structural disturbances have as their probability limits the corresponding population parameters, so that

$$\text{Plim}\frac{\Sigma U_{it}U_{jt+\delta}}{T} = V, \text{ if } \delta = 0. \tag{20}$$

The predetermined variables are also assumed to be generated by a stationary multivariate stochastic process with a non-singular contemporaneous covariance matrix V_{zz} and that any temporal dependence in the process is sufficiently weak that

$$\text{Plim}\frac{\Sigma Z_{it}Z_{jt}}{T} = V_{zz} \tag{21}$$

Also, the process generating the predetermined variables is assumed to be contemporaneously uncorrelated with the process generating the disturbances, so that

$$E(Z_{it}, U_{jt}) = 0$$

and that any temporal dependence in each of the processes is sufficiently weak that

$$\text{Plim}\frac{\Sigma Z_t U'_{t+\delta}}{T} = 0 \text{ which implies } E(U_t) = 0. \tag{22}$$

---

[4]A stochastic process is simply (E_t, $t \varepsilon T$), which is an arbitrary infinite family of real random variables. A stationary stochastic process is one whose distributions are invariant under the translation of the time. Markov processes are stochastic processes without after effect. See for example, Lajos Jakacs, *Stochastic Processes*, trans. by P. Zador (New York: John Wiley and Sons, 1960), 137 pp.

However, $E(U_t) = 0$ is not necessarily the condition of the conditional expectation of Y given Z, $E(Y_t/Z_t) = -A^{-1}BZ_t$. When assumption (22) fails, the problems raised are quite different. This assumption is of such crucial importance as really to be the defining characteristic of predetermined variables.

A similar assumption cannot be consistently made about the endogenous variables, which are clearly influenced by the disturbances. Using the reduced form (23) below and the assumption just made,

$$\text{Plim}\frac{\Sigma Y_t U'_t}{T} = M\ \text{Plim}\frac{\Sigma Z_t U'_t}{T} + \text{Plim}\frac{\Sigma w_t w'_t}{T}$$
$$= A^{-1}\ \text{Plim}\frac{\Sigma U_t U'_t}{T}$$

which, in the stochastic case, cannot generally be assumed even to have particular elements zero without further assumptions regarding the elements of A and the variance-covariance matrix of the disturbances.

Because A and B are (gxg) and (gxk) matrices of non-stochastic structural coefficients, respectively, some of whose elements may be specified a priori to be zero where A is a non-singular matrix, the reduced form of (17) can be obtained by solving it for the jointly dependent variables,

$$Y = -A^{-1}\ BZ_t + A^{-1}U_t \qquad (23)$$
$$= MZ_t + W_t$$

where

$$M = A^{-1}B = a\ \text{(gxk) matrix of reduced form coefficients}$$

$$W_t = A^{-1}U_t = a\ \text{g-order column vector of the reduced form disturbances.}$$

The statement, $M = -A^{-1}B$, means generally that each reduced form coefficient is a function of all the structural coefficients in A and in one column of B. Each reduced form disturbance W_t is a linear function of all contemporaneous structural disturbances. Simply, W_t is a linearly independent combination of U_t. This important theorem is due to Harald Cramer.[5] Therefore, assumptions about U_t are held on W_t as follows:

$$E(W_t) = E(A^{-1}U_t) \qquad (24)$$
$$= A^{-1}E(U_t) = 0 \text{ because } E(U_t) = 0$$

[5]"Any number of linear functions of normally distributed variables are themselves normally distributed... any marginal distribution of a normal distribution is itself normal, is included as particular case in this position. " Harald Cramer, *Mathematical Methods of Statistics* (Princeton: Princeton University Press, 1946), p. 313.

(25)
$$\begin{aligned} E(W_t W'_t) &= E(A^{-1}U_t) \quad (A^{-1}U_t)' \\ &= A^{-1}E(U_t U'_t)A'^{-1} \\ &= A^{-1}V\,A'^{-1} = \bar{V}'' \text{ when } t = t' \\ &= 0 \quad \text{when } t \neq t' \end{aligned}$$

Then, as it was in the structural form,

(27)
$$\text{Plim}\frac{\Sigma W_t W'_t}{T} = \bar{V}''$$

(28)
$$\text{Plim}\frac{\Sigma Z_t W'_t}{T} = 0$$

The characteristic feature of the reduced form, then, is that each equation has only *one* endogenous variable on the left-hand side and all predetermined variables on the right-hand side of the equation—vector regression scheme. The current endogenous variables are regarded as jointly dependent on all the predetermined variables of the system.

In the ID-system, only the reduced form (23) can be specified as a conditional expectation, subject to random disturbance. The structural form (17) cannot, in general, be specified as a conditional expectation. The g-structural relations of (17) "play only the role of theoretical tools by which to derive the prediction equations, "[6] i.e., (23).

If an emphasis of econometric model-building and analysis focuses on the predictive purpose of economic behaving units or sectors, then specification of model (17) has value only as an auxiliary device or theoretical tool so as to devise (23) for predictive inference. The reduced form (23) can be derived not only by the structural form (17) but by many other structural forms. This fact is not to deny that the structural model is important in its own in answering certain questions.

E. g., in an experimental situation in which governmental planning can fix a price or quantity of goods, the structural form of the ID-system can be specified as a conditional expectation.[7] However, it can intuitively be realized simply as a shift of emphasis due to estimation techniques. A rigorous argument is presented in the next section below. An essential characteristic of the ID-system discussed above can be seen easily by the simplest cobweb model,[8] in which the functional form can be specified

---

[6]Haavelmo, "The Statistical Implications of a System of Simultaneous Equations, " p. 11.

[7]*Ibid.,* p. 11–12.

[8]An excellent review on the theory was done by Mordecai Ezekiel, "The Cobweb Theorem, " *Quarterly Journal of Economics,* LII (February, 1938), 255–280.

as producers' behavior, $S_t = S(P_{t-1})$, consumers' behavior, $D_t = D(P_t)$, and the assumption of an instantaneous adjustment to equilibrium within each period t, $D_t = S_t$.[9] Then the reduced form can be expressed as $P_t = D^{-1}S(P_{t-1})$.[10] Thus the transformation involves one or more inversions of the behavioral relations.

Furthermore because of the very nature of the ID-system, the identification problem arises when the transformation of the reduced form coefficificient into a structural coefficient is not a one-to-one transformation. The problem of identification, on the other hand, is conventional and well-known. This paper will not involve such matters, but as points of interest, some essential research papers on the problem are noted as references.[11]

B. THE DILEMMA OF THE ID-SYSTEM

When an econometrician launches an interesting, if not an accurate, attack on the ID-system, it is not difficult to recall Mrs. Joan Robinson's criticism charging the econometrician with "looking in a dark room for a

---

[9]This direction of the empirical measurement is perhaps due to Henry L. Moore, in his "Empirical Laws of Demand and Supply and the Flexibility of Prices," *Political Science Quarterly,* XXXIV (December, 1919), 546–567 and "A Moving Equilibrium of Demand and Supply," *Quarterly Journal of Economics,* XXXIX (May, 1925), 357–371. Cf. Henry Schultz, "The Meaning of Statistical Demand Curves," University of Chicago February, 1930, pp. 11–24. (Mimeographed)

[10]This equation is quite legitimate in terms of a deterministic or disturbance-free model; however, argument on this point will be developed later in depth, depending upon mathematical statistics and probability theory as well as economic theories.

[11]T. C. Koopmans et al., "Measuring the Equation Systems of Dynamic Economics," in *Statistical Inference in Dynamic Economic Models,* ed. by T. C. Koopmans. Cowles' Commission for Research in Economics Monograph No. 14; (New York: John Wiley & Sons, 1950), pp. 69–110; Leonid Hurwicz, "Generalization of the Concept of Identification," in *ibid.,* pp. 238–244; Tjalling C. Koopmans, "Identification Problems in Economic Model Construction," in *Studies in Econometric Method,* ed. by William C. Hood and T. C. Koopmans Cowles Commission for Research in Economics Monograph No. 14 (New York: John Wiley & Sons, 1953), pp. 27–48; and Franklin M. Fisher. "Generalization of the Rank and Order Conditions for Identifiability," *Econometrica,* (July, 1959), 431–447.

Franklin M. Fisher presents the best unified treatment of the theory of identification in simultaneous equation estimation, including nonlinear cases, in his *The Identification Problem in Econometrics* (New York: McGraw-Hill, 1966), 203 pp.

black cat which (has already) left. "[12] Perhaps if we throw a little light on the subject we will find the room filled with traps, if we view the "room" as the ID-system. Whether or not the ID-system functions is not important here. There are enough empirical results gathered by its advocates to support the ID-system as the best approach to structural model-building. What is important to this discussion are the strong doubts some scholars raise about the "perfect" ID-system.

It behooves the econometrician, even at the risk of his reputation, to look for "a black cat. "

The econometrician cannot avoid it; he must examine—indeed scrutinize—the theoretical dilemma inherent in the ID-system and weigh the relevancy of structural model-building by alternative systems.

Dilemma I—Assumption of Equilibrium. Haavelmo, in his presidential address at the Econometric Society meeting in 1957, stated that "the concrete results of our efforts at quantitative measurement often seem to get worse the more refinement of tools and logical stringency we call into play! ... the 'laws' of economics are not very accurate in the sense of close fit, and that we have been living in a dream-world of large but somewhat superficial or spurious correlations. "[13]

In 1960, Mrs. Robinson, in discussing Haavelmo's statement said:

> the main trouble . . . has arisen from the dependence of economic theory as it is usually expounded upon the concept of equilibrium. . . . It means that every individual who has any power to change his behavior is content not to make any change. . . any actual event occurs in an out-of-equilibrium situation. . .
>
> But how can a discussion of equilibrium positions ever throw up generalizations to be confronted with statistical evidence from the out-of-equilibrium world?
>
> Theoretical model builders . . . most often try to evade the difficulty by proceeding as though we could assume that equilibrium normally prevails.[14]

Clearly, the ID-system is inspired and formalized from a very general principle of Walras-Keynes—that is, all economic variables or relations are interdependently determined by a complete set of structural equations

---

[12]Her paper, "The Choice of Model, " was presented at the Royal Statistical Society Seminar on *The Present Position of Econometrics*, April 27, 1960. See *Journal of the Royal Statistical Society* (Series A), 123, Part III (1960), pp. 274–278, especially p. 274.

[13]Trygve Haavelmo, "The Role of the Econometrician in the Advancement of Economic Theory, " *Econometrica*, XXVI (July, 1958), 355.

[14]Robinson, "The Choice of Model, " p. 375f.

under the assumption of equilibrium within an arbitrarily closed system. Furthermore, the ID-system theoretically indicates that the economy should not be studied without having detailed and accurate theory about the entire structure.

Technically speaking, the theoretical rationale of the ID-system is reversible and symmetric under the assumption of equilibrium; therefore, there are problems in assessing the notion of behavioral relations, which are the basic materials for the building of models. That is, the structural form, which is built from economic theory, has no operational meaning. It plays the role of a theoretical tool to mechanically derive the reduced form of equations, in order to provide an explicit theoretical statement from which the reduced form may be derived. However, the same reduced form can be derived from many different structural forms so that it is impossible to say which structural form is, a priori, the true one among the many.

Thus, equilibrium may be substantially destructive to the theoretical meaning of the economic behavioral equations. Furthermore, if an incorrect variable is involved in one equation it may distort the coefficients of other equations due to their simultaneity. Finally, the probability of multi-collinearity and autocorrelation is higher in the reduced form than in its counterpart, the structural form.

Dilemma II—Is it Legitimate to Modify a Model in Order to Satisfy the Existing Techniques of Estimation? Any model should be constructed in the light of the subject matter theory.

When the ID-system was initiated, the ID-school had an inclination to build just-identified structural models, mainly guided by the only existing estimating techniques; when the limited information likelihood method was introduced, over-identified models began to appear in the construction of structural models. When Theil's two-stage least-squares method (TS-LS)[15] produced propitious results in the estimation of over-identified parameters, over-identified model-building became an almost formal property of the structure.

For example, Klein in his *Economic Fluctuations* expressed his concern that the work might give the impression that he had manipulated the construction of the structural equations in terms of identification problems.

---

[15]Henry Theil, *Economic Forecasts and Policy*, 2d. rev. ed. (Amsterdam: North-Holland, 1961), pp. 225–31 and 334–44. Similar but independent work is done by R. L. Basmann, "A Generalized Classical Method of Linear Estimation of Coefficients in a Structural Equation," *Econometrica*, XXV (January, 1957), 77–83.

> The reader must not get the impression that economic theory is called upon at this moment in order to achieve identification. . . . if we fail to get an identified system because certain variables have been omitted from the equations or because the equations are not true . . . If the truth permits identification of parameters, we may proceed with statistical estimation.[16]

A more detailed method of model construction to meet identifiability criteria based on economic theory has been explained by Koopmans,[17] where he modifies Ezekiel's investment equations by introducing specific explanatory variables in sufficient numbers. This methodology is a more or less hit and miss method of model construction. At best, the approach is applicable only in a limited sense, as in the classical way of counting the number of equations and unknowns, which is neither sound deduction nor legitimate induction in econometric model-building.

Indeed, econometric model-building should logically begin with a priori economic theory and move from there to a model consistent with that theory. Later, the model can be rationally complemented with a posteriori theory if necessary. In short, the scientific models should be a joint construction of theoretical knowledge and empirical information, so as to attempt to synthesize the antithesis nature of theory and observation.

Dilemma III—The Problem of Under-Identified Models. Liu has argued that the complex economic reality makes "all structural relationships" likely to be under-identified rather than over-identified as the Cowles' researchers claim, because so many variables influence the dependent variables. "Artificial" over-identification of a model, Liu has said, is mainly due to estimating techniques rather than economic theory or a priori information.[18]

Liu refers to Klein-Goldberger's *Econometric Model of U. S.* as an example of "artificially" over-identified models and claims that they are "theoretically unsound" and ought to be rejected.[19] Liu further claims that the under-identified model is more realistic in light of the socio-economic structural system. As a matter of fact, the thought of a socio-

---

[16]Lawrence R. Klein, *Economic Fluctuations in the United States, 1921–1941,* Cowles Commission for Research in Economics Monograph No. 11. (New York: John Wiley & Sons, 1950), p. 10 including footnote 12.

[17]Koopmans, "Identification Problems in Economic Model Construction," pp. 40–44.

[18]Ta-Chung Liu, "Underidentification, Structural Estimation, and Forecasting," *Econometrica*, XXVIII (October, 1960), 856.

[19]*Ibid.*, p. 860. Cf. Mordecai Ezekiel and Karl A. Fox warned against manipulation of models for identification in their *Methods of Correlation and Regression Analysis,* 3d. ed. (New York: John Wiley & Sons, 1959), p. 431.

economic structural system, instead of thc conventional closed economic system, had had a long-standing place in evolutionary or institutional economics.[20]

Dilemma IV—An Operational Meaning of Economic Theory. Marshall's diagrammatic method of estimating demand elasticity (price elasticity) has been mathematically formulated and applied widely in economic theory,[21] in spite of Paul A. Samuelson's discredit of the Marshallian concept of elasticity coefficients as "dimensionless" and unimportant, "except possibly as mental exercises for beginning students. "[22] For instance, Allen defined it as "the elasticity of the function $Y = f(X)$ at the point X is the rate of proportional change in Y per unit proportional change in X. "[23] (Where Y is a quantity demanded and X is its corresponding prices.) Symbolically, then $E = d(\log Y)/d(\log X) = (X/Y)\ (dY/dX)$.

The ID-system's reversibility and symmetry property treats the inverse demand function as a price elasticity rather than "price flexibility, "[24] i.e., the reciprocal of the price elasticity. It is correct in a deterministic (mathematical) equation; however, it is wrong in a stochastic equation except in the case of perfect correlation. The Marshallian concept of price elasticity coefficients can be misinterpreted in a stochastic equation according to the ID-system.

Although a proof of its incorrectness is actually elementary, it may not be worthless to repeat here, because it is closely related to the 1920's and 1930's intensive debate on regression analysis which, in turn is inherited by the ID-system without a satisfactory solution, contrary to popular belief. Assuming the linearity of the relation, we can write,

$$(1) \qquad Y_t = aX_t + b + U_t \qquad (t = 1,2,\ldots T)$$

$$(2) \qquad X_t = AY_t + B + w_t$$

---

[20]For a concept of evolutionary or institutional economics, for example, see K. William Kapp, "In Defense of Institutional Economics, " *Swedish Journal of Economics*, LXX (March, 1968), 1–18.

[21]Alfred Marshall, *Principles of Economics*, 8th ed. (London: Macmillan, 1946), p. 839 and Mathematical Appendix 3.

[22]Paul A. Samuelson, *Foundations of Economic Analysis* (Cambridge: Harvard University Press, 1947), p. 125 including footnote 1. However, its concept as well as its operational meaning have been extensively and intensively used by economic theorists and econometricians including Samuelson.

[23]R. G. D. Allen, *Mathematical Analysis for Economists* (New York: St. Martin's Press, 1967), p. 251.

[24]The term "price flexibility" is initiated by Henry L. Moore, *Synthetic Economics* (New York: Macmillan, 1929), p. 38ff.

Then,

$$a = (\Sigma XY/\Sigma X^2) = r(\delta y/\delta x)$$

$$A = (\Sigma XY/\Sigma Y^2) = r(\delta x/\delta y)$$

Where, r is the coefficient of correlation; δx and δy are the standard deviations of X and Y, respectively. The price elasticity of demand from (1) is:

$$E = a(X/Y) = r\,(\delta y/\delta x)\,(X/Y)$$

and the price flexibility or the reciprocal of the elasticity from (2) is:

$$E' = A^{-1}\,(X/Y)$$

$$= r^{-1}\,(\delta y/\delta x)\,(X/Y)$$

$$\text{If } /r/ = 1,\ /E'/ = /E/.$$

$$\text{But if } /r/ \leqq 1,\ /E'/ \geqq /E/;\ \text{if } /r/ \neq 1,\ /E'/ \neq /E/.$$

Because, in regression analysis, perfect correlation is only a special case—a to A or A to a transformation is impossible without a margin of error. Considering the above simple explanation, then, the reversibility of the structural form should bring a biased estimate in the ID-system.

It is well-known that Henry Schultz' monumental work on demand analysis, using time series data, shows the dual numerical values of elasticities; one with quantity and the other with price as the dependent variable.[25] As has been seen, the Frisch-Haavelmo's elasticities for milk in Norway was 0.85–3.14 by applying the diagonal regression.[26] Thus, the dualism dilemma arises due to a straight-forward application of the reversibility principle of deterministic equation to stochastic processes. In other words, this serious pitfall in regression analysis is deeply inherited by the ID-system as a compromise version in light of the joint probability law.

A proof showing the limitations of the ID-system, in terms of statistical inference and probability theory, will be developed from the simplest, elementary text illustration of a linear demand relation between price, P_t, and quantity demanded, D_t, through time series analysis.

(3) $D_t = a + bP_t$ (for a deterministic relation)

---

[25] *The Theory and Measurement of Demand* (Chicago: University of Chicago Press, 1938), especially see pp. 146–49 and Table 11, p. 261. Cf. Lawrence R. Klein, *A Textbook of Econometrics* (Evanston, Ill.: Row, Peterson & Co., 1953), pp. 282ff., for a discussion of this and related matters.

[26] Ragnar Frisch and Trygve Haavelmo, "The Demand for Milk in Norway," *Statsøkonomisk Tidskrift*, LII (1938), as quoted in Herman Wold and Lars Juréen, *Demand Analysis: A Study in Econometrics* (New York: John Wiley & Sons, 1953), pp. xi and 30.

(4) $D_t = a + bP_t + V_t$ (for a stochastic relation)

The following equations can be obtained by solving for P_t:

(5) $$P_t = b^{-1}(D_t - a)$$

(6) $$P_t = b^{-1}(D_t - a) - b^{-1}v_t$$

When the systematic part of (4) is specified as a conditional (mathematical) expectation,

(7) $$E(D_t/P_t) = a + bP_t$$

with $E(v_t) = 0$ and $E(v_t, P_t) = 0$.

However, the corresponding specification of (6) is generally impossible, i.e.,

(8) $$E(P_t/D_t) \neq b^{-1}(D_t - a)$$

unless its coefficient of determination is 1, because of joint probability distribution $r(P_tD_t) \neq 0$ with $E(D_tv_t) \neq 0$ and Prob $(v_t = 0) < 1$.

A Generalization of Dilemma IV. The matrix form of the structural form of equations (17) and the reduced form (23) in subchapter (A) of this Chapter can be expressed as,

(9) $$Y = A\bar{Y} + BZ + U$$

(Time subscript t is not shown for convenience.)

Where, "$-$" in $\bar{Y}$ denotes explanatory endogenous variables; the rest of the notations and assumptions are the same as before.

(10) $$Y = (1 - A)^{-1}BZ + (1 - A)^{-1}U$$
$$= MZ + W$$

Where, $M = (1 - A)^{-1}B$ and $W = (1 - A)^{-1}U$

If there are no stochastic values as a deterministic case, (9) and (10) are perfectly trivial just as in (3) and (5). However, the dualism arises in the stochastic case in terms of conditional expectations so as to provide predictive inference. That is,

(11) $$E(Y/MZ) = MZ$$

and implies that

(12) $E(Y/\bar{Y}, Z) \neq AY + BZ$

unless the coefficient of determination, $R^2 = 1$.

Ever since the inception of the Cowles ID-system, the dualism between (11) and (12) has been a salient point of the system. In principle, the dualism of the ID-system has a close connection with the dualism which was a focus of the regression debate of the 1920s and 1930s, as demonstrated in equations (7) and (8). The reduced form (10) involves the same problem of inversion as shown in (4) and (6). The serious theoretical and operational dilemma arises over which interpretation should be given to the coefficients a_{ij} and b_{ij} in (12), when the systematic part of (9) cannot be specified as conditional expectations.

Because of the importance of this confusion over a fundamental theory of mathematical statistics, Koopmans' demand and supply equations system with the assumption of instantaneous equilibrium[27] is presented here as a simple example illustrating the dilemma.

$$y_1 = a_{12}y_2 + b_{11}z_1 + b_{12}z_2 + b_{10} + u_1 \tag{13}$$

$$y_2 = a_{22}y_1 + b_{21}z_1 + b_{22}z_2 + b_{20} + u_2 \tag{14}$$

(Time subscript, t, is not shown for convenience.)

with $a_{12} = a_{21} = 0$ and $b_{12} \neq b_{22}$ as the a priori information.

Then, th equations of the reduced form are:

$$y_1 = m_{11}z_1 + m_{12}z_2 + m_{10} + w_1 \tag{15}$$

$$y_2 = m_{21}z_1 + m_{22}z_2 + m_{20} + w_2 \tag{16}$$

with the following specification,

$$E(y_1/z_1, z_2) = m_{11}z_1 + m_{12}z_2 + m_{10} \tag{17}$$

$$E(y_2/z_1, z_2) = m_{21}z_1 + m_{22}z_2 + m_{20} \tag{18}$$

Then, (17) and (18) imply that

$$E(y_1/y_2, z_1) \neq a_{12}y_2 + b_{11}z_1 + b_{10} \tag{19}$$

$$E(y_2/y_1, z_2) \neq a_{22}y_1 + b_{22}z_2 + b_{20} \tag{20}$$

Thus, (13) and (14) cannot be specified as conditional expectations, due to (17) and (18) for (15) and (16) unless there is a perfect correlation, $R^2 = 1$. However, paradoxically, the ID-system is based on the validity of this "dualism." If this were not so, there would be no theoretical rationale to give an interpretation for the parameters a_{ij} and b_{ij} in (13) and (14).

[27]See Tjalling C. Koopmans' third example, relations 7d and 7s, in his "Identification Problems in Economic Model Construction," p. 33.

CHAPTER IV

THE CAUSAL CHAIN (OR RECURSIVE) SYSTEM

CHAPTER IV

THE CAUSAL CHAIN (or RECURSIVE) SYSTEM[1]

In the preceding chapter it was pointed out that there exist various dilemmas in the interdependent (ID) system, in spite of the fact that the best available arsenal of modern econometric model-building and analysis has been developed in terms of the ID-system. Subsequently, it is the purpose here to probe in depth the causal chain (CC) system as an alternative approach to the ID-system. In the final analysis, this CC-system may prove to be more than an alternative approach because the dilemmas inherent in the ID-system do not exist in the CC-system.

It has been shown that the two systems are essentially the same in their formal appearance in mathematical form. The difference is only the form in which their coefficients of explanatory endogenous variables assume. A block matrix represents the ID-system; whereas, a triangular is a special case of the block matrix, expresses the CC-system. However, when we build a stochastic model, deep-going differences are bred between the two systems, particularly because of the problem of reversibility of behavior relations in the ID-system's transformation from the structural form to the reduced form. In terms of economic theory, the two systems begin to differ fundamentally based on opposing conception of reality—equi-

[1]Although the two terms, recursive and causal chain, can be used interchangeably, the former refers to the formal framework of a model without alluding to subject matter theory or information, and the latter connotes the implementation of subject matter theory in the recursive model so as to dynamize the model as a version of the vector regression scheme or the reduced form by way of the chain of iterative substitution. See Herman Wold. "Forecasting by the Chain Principle," in M. Rosenblatt (ed.), *Symposium on Time Series Analysis* (New York: John Wiley & Sons, 1963), pp. 478ff.

librium versus disequilibrium approach.

Although a model may be built to serve a particular purpose at hand, it should be designed to give an interpretation based on conditional expectations. These expectations should be subject to disturbance terms if the intention is to explain and predict behavior of economic units. Thus, the emphasis here is placed on the explanatory and predictive rationale of a model rather than on a descriptive basis, because the main purpose of economic theory, in my opinion, is to explain and to predict from certain given conditions their corresponding developments.

Before entering such technical areas, however, a few *obiter dicta* concerning the true meaning of causality in the CC-system may be in order. The historically unfortunate term "causality" is one of the major reasons for misunderstanding of the CC-system. Another misunderstanding of the system is perhaps due to an illusion that the system is established so as to employ a simple estimation technique. Consequently, after the meaning of "causality" is discussed, causality is operatively employed in section (B).

Following these explanations, it is then possible to present with understanding the theoretical and operational rationale of the CC-system in terms of Wold's synthesized version of Kolmogorov's theorem and Yule's autoregressive process. To establish a firm conviction of the soundness of the CC-system and its estimation rationale, the theoretical and operational foundations of the CC-system are developed in the form of theorems. Finally, to demonstrate the various ways of model-building, the CC-system is classified as subsystems as (1) a vector regression system and (2) a conventional causal chain system.

A. THE MEANING OF "CAUSALITY" IN THE CC-SYSTEM

The CC-system has been defined in light of the inductive hierarchy in relation to logical empiricism,[2] in order to highlight the *scientific* use of

[2]In the philosophy of science, a synthesis of theoretical and empirical procedure forms the apparent antithesis of theoretical and empirical knowledge and can be said to be an approach of logical empiricism. The antithesis of a priori theory and an empirical observation should be synthesized, e.g., as in Euclidean geometry. Of course, it is not intended to take an extreme position of any particular school of thought such as the Vienna circle or other continental schools. For example, see Alfred J. Ayer. *Language, Truth and Logic* (New York: Dover Publications, 1952), pp. 134–153.

the term "causality" as opposed to its metaphysical sense. It has also been pointed out in Chapter II, that this "causality" is a necessary condition in formulating a disequilibrium, dynamic model. "Causality" is essential in implementing the asymmetry and irreversibility characteristics of any autonomous behaving unit without affecting or being affected by the behavior of other autonomous units, at least during a certain time period.

Thus, the scientific use of causality is based upon the assumption of causal influence (asymmetry or irreversibility) more than causal inference (symmetry or reversibility). The assumption of causal influence involves the simulation of a cause-effect relation in a controlled experiment in which cause-effect or stimulus-response is designed to explain and predict, and is therefore specified by the experimenter's subject matter knowledge or theory and depends upon the purpose of the experiment. Consequently, specification of the direction of causal influence is dependent upon the experiment design to explain rather than merely describe, and upon the theory of the model.

Similarly, in a non-experimental situation, the direction of causal influence in a single relation and the flow of causation in a system of simultaneous relations, as a generalization of causal influence, are also specified by subject matter theory or a priori information about the field of application. That is, causality is a more fundamental question than problems of mathematics and statistics, including its estimation techniques.

Thus, an operational concept of causality in the CC-system is very remote from metaphysics and the concept has no kinship with the controversial "principle of efficient causality." However, the unfortunate use of the term in the CC-system as an assumption has been misunderstood, mainly because of historical and religious consequences in the philosophy of science.[3] Alternative terms such as "functional relation," "interdepen-

---

[3]The ID-school's argument against "causality" stems from a metaphysical notion. For instance, Bertrand Russell, "On the Notion of Cause, with Application to the Free-Will Problem, " in Herbert Feigl and May Brodbeck (eds.), *Readings in the Philosophy of Science* (New York: Appleton-Century-Cofts, 1952) pp. 387–407, insists on "extruding" the term "causality" from the philosophy of science. In association with this line of thought, e.g., Herbert A. Simon began to use the above alternative terms in quotation marks to emphasize the argument. See Simon's "Causal Ordering and Identifiability, " in Wm. C. Hood and Tjalling C. Koopmans (eds.) *Studies in Econometric Method* (New York: John Wiley & Sons, 1953), pp. 49–74.

With algebraic equations, Simon technically and philosophically showed that causation is simply a "functional relationship" or "interdependence" between some variables in a "self-contained structure," and hence, "it is best to abandon" the metalanguage of causality.

Commenting on Simon's discussion, Herman Wold in his "Causality and Econometrics, " *Econometrica*, XXII (April, 1954) 162–177, argued that Simon's approach is "to throw out the baby with the bathwater. "

dent relations, " or, simply, "relations" have been employed to replace the term, "causal relation."

Unfortunately, these alternative terms are not successful in explaining the formal framework of the CC-system. To put it another way, alternative terms have failed to distinguish between the operative use of causal influence and of causal inference in model-building.

(*1*) An illustrative explanation of a difference between causal influence and causal inference: In designing physical experiments of Boyle's law for ideal gas, $PV = cT$, where P is pressure; V, volume; c, constant; T, temperature; it is legitimate to arrange experiments as $P \leftarrow c(T/V)$ and $V \leftarrow c(T/P)$ in terms of causal influence. But $T \leftarrow (1/c)(PV)$ is not possible as an experimental model; i.e., T as an effect variable and PV as cause variables. Of course, it is legitimate to derive T in a causal inference sense. Thus, "functional relations" or simply "relations" is valid for all of three forms in the causal inference sense, i.e., to infer the left-hand variables when the right-hand variables are known or given. This example can be conceived as a non-controversial principle of causality in applied physics.

This principle can be defined as analogous to non-experimental phenomena for (a) an exact definite relation; (b) a behavioral relation:

(a) It is well-known that a fundamental difference between the quantity theory and the income theory begins with a causal assumption concerning the definitional equation $MV \equiv Y$, where $M =$ the money supply, $V =$ velocity of circulation, and $Y =$ flow of spending. The former develops its argument assuming MV as a cause and Y as an effect; however, the latter's assumption is that the flow of expenditures should causally explain MV. If the equation is interpreted as a "mutual relation, " or "functional relation, " and the argument becomes a matter of brain-teasing.

(b) Keynes' fundamental psychological law has a causal sense in that it is presented as $C = f(Y)$ rather than the other way around. Duesenberry's ratchet effect is more explicitly assured as an asymmetric and irreversible function with respect to changes in income. The effect may be protracted over a long-run basis—in spite of the fact that there is no explicit inclusion of a disturbance term—if there are sufficient and permanent changes in consumer habits. On the other hand, when a disturbance term is explicitly allowed into behavioral relations, the alternative terms cannot be replaced without a loss of operative use of the regression model, due to the latter's irreversibility principle.

Thus the above meaning of causality is fused to the CC-system, but not in the same sense that the historical past causes the present and the future. Restated another way, these scientific concepts of causality are employed as an assumption—resulting from a logical consequence of subject matter theory—in order for causality to be translated by probability terms and mathematical statistics into model-building. An ordinary notion of the term, cause-effect, explanatory-explained, impulse-outcome, stimulus-response, determining-determined, independent-dependent, etc., in the physical sciences, is simulated by econometric model-building. A causal assumption thus enters as a priori knowledge in model-building, so that one can explore feedback phenomena by way of causal relations rather than assume it through vague notions of interdependency derived from a very short time span[4] or aggregation of data. In addition, in the process of model-building, it is safe to assume a builder has some causal logic in mind. For example, when a person is constructing a verbal or qualitative system of equations expressing economic problems, he can be successful if the simultaneous variables, say *A*, *B*, *C*, etc., can be found in succession without the necessity of solving any simultaneous pairs of relations.

B. "CAUSALITY" IN OPERATIVE USE

In order to provide a rationale for operative use of causality, in particular causal influence, let us postulate a simple example of linear demand relations with a disturbance term, namely,

$$D_t = a + bY_t + u_t \qquad t = 1, 2, \ldots, T$$

where D is per capita quantity demanded; Y is per capita income; u is normally an independently distributed term.

If the relation is for an operative use beyond description, conditional expectation should be established as

$$E(D_t/Y_t) = a + bY_t$$

in which $E(u_t) = 0$ and $E(Y_t, u_t) = 0$ are implied.

For descriptive or causal inference, however, it may be necessary only to state that as income is increased, demand rises or vice versa. This fact

[4]A discussion of this subject is beyond the scope of this paper. For a detailed argument of the soundness of the causal chain model under these circumstances, see Enders A. Robinson, "Structural Properties of Stationary Stochastic Processes with Applications," ed. by M. Rosenblatt, *Brown University Symposium on Time Series Analysis* (New

can be stated without qualification of the conditional expectation specification. When no causality is assumed in the relation, the regression of the left-hand variable upon the right-hand variable(s) is only an average relation in the sample. On the other hand, the change in demand is explained by the change in income in terms of the conditional expectation, i.e., as Y changes by the amount $\triangle$, corresponding expected changes in D is:

$$E(D/Y \rightarrow Y + \triangle) \rightarrow D + b\triangle$$

and this notion can be straightforwardly applied in a prediction under *ceteris paribus* assumption.

Now having demonstrated through an example an essential feature of operative use of causal influence, it may be necessary to discuss a detailed way of model specification with multivariate regressors for further development of this study. Let us say that the multivariate model is:

$$y = b_0 + b_1x_1 + \ldots + b_nx_n + v$$

where y is the explained variable; x_i (i = 1,2,...,n) are the explanatory variables; and v is a disturbance term which is assumed as normally and independently distributed.

For a given x_i, conditional expectation of y,

$$E(y/x_1,\ldots,x) = b_0 + b_1x_1 + \ldots + b_nx_n$$

has an old standing from the inception of regression analysis.

According to *H*. Cramer,[5] given the joint probability distribution of $n+1$ random variables (y,x_i) for the conditional expectation of y for known values or random variables of x_i, $E(y/x_1,\ldots,x_n) + v$ can be written where the disturbance term v has the conditional expectation of zero, $E(v/x_i) = 0$. Thus, a conditional expectation can provide a rationale for several inference procedures, in dealing with jointly distributed variables. The conditional expectation implies that v is uncorrelated with conditioning variables, x_i. In symbols, $r(v,x_1) = \ldots = r(v,x_n) = 0$. Since $y = b_0 + b_ix_i + \ldots + b_nx_n + v$ and $E(y/x_i)$ implies $E(v/x_i)$ for any fixed $x_1, \ldots, x_n$, $E(v.x_i/x_1,\ldots, x_n) = 0$ for every i. And also, conditional expectations of v and $v.x_\iota$ are zero (or $E(v) = 0$ and $E(v.x_i) = 0$ since i is arbitrary).

York: John Wiley & Sons, 1963), pp. 170–192 and "Wavelet Composition of Time-Series," ed. by Herman Wold *Economettic Model Building* (Amsterdam: North-Holland, 1964), pp. 37–106; see also Herman World and Enders A. Robinson, "Minimum-Delay Structure of Least-Squares and *Eo-Ipso* Predicting Systems for Stationary Stochastic Processes," in *Symposium on Time Series Analysis*, pp. 192–196.

[5]Harald Cramer, *Mathematical Methods of Statistics* (Princeton, N. J.; Princeton University Press, 1946), pp. 260–290, 301–310, and 548–556.

In accordance with these ideas, the specification of the causal hypothesis must be established in agreement with the subject matter theory before the statistical techniques can be put into action. Once this type of specification is completed, the method of least-squares regression thus adopts clear legitimacy as does its estimation of parameters, particularly in the sense of causal influence. Since the regression is actually a tool of subject matter analysis—serving to explain the variations in the left-hand variable as the effect of variations in the right-hand cause variables—the regression forms a hypothetical explanation of the effect variable for the phenomenon under analysis and provides a measure of how the effect variable is influenced by the cause variables.

Furthermore, as was developed for one regressor case of our example above, the changes in y are explained and predicted under a *ceteris paribus* assumption by the change in any x_i or all x_i in terms of the conditional expectation by which as x_i changes by the amount $\triangle$, corresponding expected changes in y become:

(1) $E(y/x_1 \to x_1 + \triangle_1, x_2,\ldots,x_n) = b_0 + b_1(x_1 + \triangle_1) +$

$b_2x_2 \ldots + b_nx_n = y + b_1\triangle_1$

(2) $E(y_1/x_1 \to x_1 + \triangle_1, x_2 + \triangle_2, x_3,\ldots,x_n) = b_0 +$

$b_1(x_1 + \triangle_1) + b_2(x_2 + \triangle_2) + b_3x_3 + \ldots + b_nx_n =$

$y + b_1\triangle_1 + b_2\triangle_2$

. . . .

(n) $E(y/x_1 \to x_1 + \triangle_1,\ldots,x_n \to x_n + \triangle_n) =$

$y + b_1\triangle_1 + \ldots + b_n\triangle_n$

....

$(n + m)$ ....

In the above, any arbitrary i or any arbitrary number of combinations of i can also be easily seen.

Although the above discussion is based on a unirelational model to explain the operative use of causality, the causality can be also easily generalized in a system of simultaneous equations. The generalization is followed while more theories and technical matters are developed below.

C. THEORETICAL RATIONALE AND OPERATIONAL IMPLICATION OF THE CC-SYSTEM

The CC-system as defined in Chapter II can easily be generalized as follows:

$$
\text{(I)}\quad
\begin{aligned}
&(1) \quad y_1 = a_{11}y_1 + \dots + a_{1h}y_h + b_{11}z_1 + \dots + b_{1m}z_m + v_1 \\
&(2) \quad y_2 = a_{21}y_1 + \dots + a_{2h}y_h + b_{21}z_1 + \dots + b_{2m}z_m + v_2 \\
&\dots\dots\dots\dots\dots\dots\dots\dots\dots\dots\dots\dots \\
&(h) \quad y_h = a_{h1}y_1 + \dots + a_{hh}y_h + b_{h1}z_1 + \dots + b_{hm}z_m + v_h
\end{aligned}
$$

(Time subscripts are not shown for convenience.)

where, $a_{ij} = 0$ if $i \leqq j$. (It is subdiagonalization of coefficients of explanatory endogenous variables)

y_i (with $i = 1,2,\dots,h$) = endogenous variables

z_j (with $j = 1,2,\dots,m$) = predetermined variables which contain lagged endogenous and exogenous variables and unlagged exogenous variables

v_i (with $i = 1,2,\dots,h$) = the residual terms with homoscedasticity assumptions

The system (I) can be expressed in a compact matrix form as,

$$\text{(II)} \qquad Y = \bar{A}Y + BZ + V$$

where "–" in $\bar{A}$ indicates $a_{ij} = 0$ when $i \leqq j$ in $\bar{A}$ (or a priori zero coefficients of Y).

$$
\bar{A} = \begin{bmatrix} 0 & 0 & 0 & 0 \dots\dots 0 \\ a_{21} & 0 & 0 & 0 \dots\dots 0 \\ a_{31} & a_{32} & 0 & 0 \dots\dots 0 \\ \dots & \dots & \dots & \dots\dots 0 \\ a_{h1} & a_{h2} \dots & a_{h,h-1} & 0 \end{bmatrix}; \quad
B = \begin{bmatrix} b_{11} & \dots & b_{1m} \\ \dots & \dots & \dots \\ b_{h1} & \dots & b_{hm} \end{bmatrix};
$$

$$Y' = (y_1 y_2 \dots y_h);\ Z' = (z_1 z_2 \dots z_m);\ V' = (v_1 v_2 \dots v_h)$$

The reduced form is,

(III) $$Y = (I - \bar{A})^{-1} BZ + (I - \bar{A})^{-1} V = MZ + w$$

where $M = (I - \bar{A})^{-1} B;\ w = (I - \bar{A})^{-1} V$

$$M = \begin{bmatrix} m_{11} & 0 & 0 & 0 & \dots & 0 \\ m_{21} & m_{22} & 0 & 0 & \dots & 0 \\ m_{31} & m_{32} & m_{33} & 0 & \dots & 0 \\ \dots & \dots & \dots & \dots & \dots & 0 \\ \dots & \dots & \dots & \dots & \dots & 0 \\ m_{h1} & m_{h2} & m_{h3} & & \dots & m_{hh} \end{bmatrix}$$

As was demonstrated in Chapter II (B), relation (6a), the reduced form (III) is derived by a chain of iterative substitution in terms of the sub-diagonal matrix $\bar{A}$. Simply, the right-hand side of (I–1) is substituted for y_1 in (I–2), the right-hand side of (I–2) is again substituted for y_2 in (I–3), and so on until (I-h) equation. Therefore, the structural form (I) and the reduced form (III) are isomorphous, i.e., mathematically and stochastically equivalent.

An operational rationale of the chain substitution processes of the CC-system is congruous with Wold's synthesized theorem. His theorem is based on Kolmogorov's fundamental lemma—"expectations of conditional expectations yield non-conditional expectations"[6]—and on Yule's autoregressive process.[7] Its essential feature is developed as follows:

(I-1-a) $$y_1^* = E(y_1/z_1,\dots,z_m)$$

(I-1-b) $$= b_{11}z_1 + \dots + b_{1m}z_m$$

Equation (I–1), whose endogenous variable y_1 is causally explained

---

[6]Wold, "Forecasting by the Chain Principle," pp. 13–14. Actually, Wold's theorem is implied in his *A Study in the Analysis of Stationary Time Series* 1938, 2d. ed., (Uppsala, Sweden: Almqvist & Wiksells, 1954), pp. 101–103. Cf. A. N. Kolmogorov, *Foundations of the Theory of Probability,* 1933, trans. by Nathan Morrison, 2d. English ed. (New York: Chelsea, 1950), pp. 52–56.

[7]The autoregressive process is simply known as Yule's process in Herman Wold, *A Study in the Analysis of Stationary Time Series,* pp. 24–32.

Cf. G. U. Yule, in his "on a Method of Investigating Periodicities in Distributed Series, with Special Reference to Wolfer's Sunspot Numbers," *Philosophical Transactions*, Royal Society CCXXVI, 267–298, described a linear difference equation, in which $Y = aY_{t-1} + bY_{t-2} + \dots = aY_{t-1} + bY_{t-2} + U_t$. The equation depicts the wavelike but not strictly periodic change in sunspot frequency or density which resembles the movements of a damped pendulum kept moving by random shocks.

by solely predetermined variables, z_j ($j = 1,2,\ldots,m$), can be specified as the conditional expectation in accordance with the above section. Thus $y_1^* = E(y_1/z_1,\ldots,z_m)$. This specification implies $E(v_1/z_i) = 0$; for every i. In addition, $E(v_1) = 0$ and $E(v_1 z_i) = 0$ since i is arbitrary. Because the hypothetical relation is specified as a conditional expectation, the least-squares estimators can predict consistent and efficient estimates of parameters.

Now having developed equation (I–1), the chain of iterative substitution can be unfolded step by step. In **the first step**: y_1^* is substituted for y_1 in (I–2) and yields

(I-2-a) $$y_2 = \tilde{a}_{21} y_1^* + b_{21} z_1 + \ldots + b_{2m} z_m + v_2^*;$$

where the tilde above a_{21} and asterisk beside v_2 are employed to denote theoretically transformed values of a_{21} and v_2 and are necessitated by the substitution of y_1^* for y_1. The asterisk is intended to show that y_1^* is independent of v_2^*. (This theme is parallel to theorem 1 below.)

Also the following relations can be established:

(I–2-a)″ $$y_2 = \tilde{a}_{21} E(y_1/z_1,\ldots,z_m) + b_{21} z_1 + \ldots + b_{2m} z_m + v_2^* \text{ since (I-1-a)}$$

$$= (\tilde{a}_{21} b_{11} + b_{21})\, z_1 + (\tilde{a}_{21} b_{12} + b_{22}) z_2 + \ldots +$$

$$(\tilde{a}_{21} b_{1m} + b_{2m}) + v_2^* \text{ since (I-1-b).}$$

It is justifiable, as a consequence, to conclude that y_2 is causally explained by y_1^* and $z_1,\ldots,z_m$ and, in turn, it is equally justifiable to specify the relation (I–2-a) in terms of conditional expectations, i.e.,

(I–2-b) $$y_2^* = E(y_2/y_1^*, z_1,\ldots,z_m)$$

(I–2-c) $$= \tilde{a}_{21} y_1^* + b_{21} z_1 + \ldots + b_{2m} z_m$$

(I–2-d) $$= \tilde{a}_{21} E(y_1/z_1,\ldots,z_m) + b_{21} z_1 + \ldots + b_{2m} z_m \text{ since (I–1-a)}$$

(I–2-e) $$= (\tilde{a}_{21} b_{11}) z_1 + (\tilde{a}_{21} b_{12} + b_{22}) + \ldots + (\tilde{a}_{21} b_{1m} + b_{2m}) z_m \text{ since (I–1-b)}$$

The second step: y_2^* is substituted for y_2 in (I–3).
Then,

(I–3-a) $$y_3 = \tilde{a}_{31} y_1^* + \tilde{a}_{32} y_2^* + b_{31} z_1 + \ldots + b_{3m} z_m + v_3^*$$

(I–3-a)″ $$= \tilde{a}_{31} E(y_1/z_1,\ldots,z_m) + \tilde{a}_{32} E(y_2/y_1^*, z_1,\ldots,z_m) + b_{31} z_1 + \ldots +$$

$$b_{3m} z_m + v_3^* \text{ since (I-1-a) and (I–2-a)}$$

$$= [\tilde{a}_{31} b_{11} + \tilde{a}_{32}(\tilde{a}_{21} b_{11} + b_{21}) + b_{31}] z_1 + \ldots +$$

$$[\tilde{a}_{31} b_{2m} + \tilde{a}_{32}(\tilde{a}_{21} + b_{2m}) + b_{3m}] z_m + v_3^*$$

since (I–1-a) and (I–1-b).

Therefore, y_3 can be causally explained by y_1^*, y_2^*, and $z_1,\ldots,z_m$ and the relation can be specified as a conditional expectation as before. Hence,

(I–3-b) $y_3^* = E(y_3/y_1^*, y_2^*, z_1,\ldots,z_m)$

(I–3-c) $= \tilde{a}_{31}y_1^* + \tilde{a}_{32}y_2^* + b_{31}z_1 + \ldots + b_{3m}z_m$

(I–3-d) $= \tilde{a}_{31}E(y_1/z_1,\ldots,z_m) + \tilde{a}_{32}E(y_2/y_1^*z_1,\ldots z_m) + b_{31}z_1 + \ldots + b_{3m}z_m$ since (I–1-a) and (I–2-a)

$= \tilde{a}_{31}E(y_1/z_1,\ldots,z_m) + \tilde{a}_{32}E[y_2/E(y_2/z_1,\ldots,z_m), z_1,\ldots,z_m] + b_{31}z_1 + \ldots + b_{3m}z_m$

Since (I–1-a) and Kolmogorov's theorem,

(I–3-e) $= \tilde{a}_{31}(b_{11}z_1 + b_{1m}z_m) + \tilde{a}_{32}\,[(\tilde{a}_{21}b_{11} + b_{21})z_1 + \ldots + (\tilde{a}_{21}b_{1m} + b_{2m})]\,z_m$ since (I–1-a) and (I–2-e)

$= (\tilde{a}_{31}b_{11} + \tilde{a}_{32}\tilde{a}_{21}b_{11} + \tilde{a}_{32}b_{21})z_1 + \ldots + (\tilde{a}_{31}b_{1m} + \tilde{a}_{32}\tilde{a}_{21}b_{1m} + \tilde{a}_{32}b_{2m})z_m$

This step by step chain of substitution can be extended until the step, (I-h), in which y_{h-1}^* is substituted for y_h in (I-h), and then,

The last step, (I-h):

(I-h-a) $y_h = \tilde{a}_{h1}y_1^* + \ldots + \tilde{a}_{h,\,h-1}y_{h-1} + b_{h1}z_1 + \ldots + b_{hm}z_m + v_h^*$

(I-h-a)″ $= \tilde{a}_{h1}E(y_1/z_1,\ldots,z_m) + \ldots + \tilde{a}_{h,\,h-1}E(y_{h-1}/z_1,\ldots,z_m) + b_{h1}z_1 + \ldots + b_{hm}z_m + v_h^*.$

Therefore, y_h can be explained causally by $y_1^*,\ldots,y_{h-1}^*$, $z_1,\ldots,z_m$ and the relation (I-h-a) can be specified in terms of conditional expectation, namely,

(I-h-b) $y_h^* = E(y_1^*,\ldots,y_{h-1}^*,z_1,\ldots,z_m)$

(I-h-c) $= \tilde{a}_{h1}y^* + \ldots + \tilde{a}_{h,\,h-1}y_{h-1}^* + b_{h1}z_1 + \ldots + b_{hm}z_m.$

The above equations are sufficient for our purposes without further algebric development of the relation.

The above demonstration serves a dual function: to choose an appropriate method of estimation technique; and to rationalize the chosen method by a system of simultaneous equations, in terms of Wold's theorem and corollaries to the original theorem. However, prior to further development of the above theme, some transitional statements are included below as a logical consequence.

Having completed the theoretical chain of iterative substitution, it can be concluded that system (I) and the derived system of equations are isomorphous, i.e., mathematically and stochastically equivalent. Consequently, both the "direct" and "indirect" methods of the least-squares regression analysis can lead to consistent estimates of the structural parameters. The terms, "direct" and "indirect" methods, are employed here to represent the least-squares application in the series of equations (I-i-a), where i=1,2,...,h, and the least-squares application in the series of equations (I-i-a)″, respectively.

Furtheremore, the direct least-squares estimator is the optimum in the sense that it is practically the same as the full-information maximum-likelihood-estimator in system (I). In this system, the likelihood function (L) for the disturbance terms v_i $(i = 1,2,\ldots,h)$ at time t $(t = 1,2,\ldots,T)$ is

$$L = (2\pi)^{-hT/2} \; (\delta_1\delta_2\ldots\delta_h)^T EXP\left[- \tfrac{1}{2}\Sigma(v_1{}^2/\delta_1{}^2 + \ldots + v^2{}_h/\delta^2{}_h)\right].$$

Here the Jacobian transformation of v_i into $y_1,\ldots,y_h$ is

$$J = \begin{vmatrix} \partial v_1/\partial y_1 & \ldots & \partial v_1/\partial y_h \\ \vdots & & \\ \partial v_h/\partial y_1 & \ldots & \partial v_h/\partial y_h \end{vmatrix}$$

$$= \begin{vmatrix} 1 & 0 & \ldots & 0 \\ -a_{11} & 1 & \ldots & 0 \\ \cdot & & & \cdot \\ \cdot & \cdot & & \\ \cdot & & \cdot & \cdot \\ -a_{h1} & -a_{h2} & \ldots & 1 \end{vmatrix} = 1$$

Then,

$$\text{Log L} = \text{Constant} + \text{T Log}\ \delta_1\ldots\delta_h - \tfrac{1}{2}\Sigma(v_1{}^2/\delta_1{}^2 + \ldots + v_h{}^2/\delta_h{}^2).$$

Therefore, the minimization of variances (or the least-squares method) is isomorphous to the maximization of the function. These estimates are consistent with each other, in the sense that they converge with probabilities of 1 regarding the true values extrapolated from infinitely large samples. The estimates are also equally efficient, in the sense that they have variances which never exceed those of other normally distributed estimates from large samples.

Although the direct and the indirect least-squares methods lead to consistent estimates of the system (I) due to their isomorphism, the former is a superior[8] method to the latter. This superiority is due to the fact that the direct method, in general, has smaller variances than the indirect method in view of the Schwartz inequality,[9] e.g., $(\Sigma XY)^2 \leqq \Sigma X^2 \Sigma Y^2$. Furthermore, the latter in practice has more serious problems, such as that of identification in the process of transforming the subject into the space within the structural parameters.

With knowledge of the comparative functions of the direct and indirect methods of the least-squares regression, it is now possible to discuss additional rationale of the CC-system. A second essential rationale of the chain substitution processes is derived from Wold's famous proximity theorem, particularly, in terms of his dwindling correlatedness assumption between the explanatory endogenous variables and the disturbance terms in the probability limit. For example, in symbols:

$$\text{Plim}(y_{1t}v_{1t})/T \cong 0 \text{ in (I-2)}$$

The Proximity Theorem:[10] If either (A)-the disturbance terms are small; or (B)-the probability limits of the correlation between the disturbance and the explanatory endogenous variables approach zero—the conventional least-squares method remains consistent. That is, the least-squares estimator approaches consistency whether the variance of the disturbance term approaches zero or whether the probability limit of the correlation between the disturbance term and the regressors approaches zero. The conditions, (A) and (B), reinforce each other.

In Wold's example[11] of the reinforcement of (A) and (B): let the theoretical relation be $D = BP + u$, where all variables are recorded as deviations from the mean value and let the empirical relation by the least-squares method be $D = bP + v$ with $E(P) = E(D) = 0$. Then, if $\delta(u) = 0.2\ \delta(P)$ and $r(P, u) = 0.2$, $E(b) = E(PD)/E(P^2) = B + E(Pu)/E(P^2) = B + r(P,u)\delta(u)/\delta(p) = B + 0.04$. Because of the reinforcement of (A) and (B), the bias of b is only 0.04 and provides the basis for the argument for dwindling correlatedness between the explanatory endogenous variables and the disturbance term in the probability limit.

Originally, as is widely known, the proximity theorem has been the basic theorem in the study of specification error, with rigorous proof

---

[8]For an interesting comparison with the ID-propagator's hasty conjecture, see p.43, Chapter III.

[9]Wold and Jureen, *Demand Analysis*, pp. 187–188; also see E. Malinvaud, *Statistical Methods of Econometrics* (Chicago: Rand McNally, 1966), pp. 542–543.

[10]Wold and Jureen, *Ibid.*, pp. 187–192 and Wold and P. Faxer, "On the Specification Error in Regression Analysis," *Annals of Mathematical Statistics*, XXVIII (March, 1957), 265–267.

[11]Wold and Jureen, *Ibid.*, p. 37.

coming from Wold and others. In their proof, it is apparent that the proximity theorem can be extended to apply to the CC-system as a corollary to Wold's theorem. This author originally intended to include the following theorem in the above chain of iterative substitution processes, but preferred to postpone its presentation until this point.

Theorem *1*: The explanatory endogenous variables in their structural form can be operationally assumed as independent variables, if they can be replaced by calculated values of those variables. Then the method of least-squares regression can be directly applied to each relation in the system *sériatim*, after the explanatory endogenous variables are replaced by the calculated values of those variables.

Technically, theorem 1 is $E(\ddot{Y}, V^*) = 0$, even if $E(Y, V) = |\varepsilon| > 0$, in system (I), where $|\varepsilon|$ is an arbitrarily small constant; umlaut on Y denotes calculated values of the explanatory endogenous variables; the asterisk denotes a different value of V after the right-hand side of Y is substituted by $\ddot{Y}$.

Proof of $E(\ddot{Y}, V^*) = 0$ *even if* $E(Y, V) > 0$ *or* $= |\varepsilon| > 0$:

When Y is replaced by $\ddot{Y}$ in accordance with the subdiagonal matrix, $\bar{A}$,

$$\begin{aligned} Y &= \bar{A}Y + BZ + V \\ &= \bar{A}\ddot{Y} + BZ + V^* \end{aligned}$$

$$\text{where } E(Y/\ddot{Y}, Z) = \bar{A}\ddot{Y} + BZ.$$

Then,

$$\begin{aligned} \bar{A}Y + V &= \bar{A}\ddot{Y} + V^* \\ V^* &= \bar{A}Y - \bar{A}\ddot{Y} + V \end{aligned}$$

$$\text{since } Y = (I - \bar{A})^{-1}BZ + (I - \bar{A})^{-1}V \text{ and}$$

$$\ddot{Y} = E(Y/Z) = (I - \bar{A})^{-1}BZ.$$

Hence:

$$\begin{aligned} V^* &= \bar{A}[(I - \bar{A})^{-1}BZ + (I - \bar{A})^{-1}V - (I - \bar{A})^{-1}BZ] + V \\ &= \bar{A}(I - \bar{A})^{-1}V + V \\ &= [\bar{A}(I - \bar{A})^{-1} + I]V \\ &= (I - \bar{A})^{-1}V \end{aligned}$$

$$\text{where } E(Z_i, Z_j) = 0 \quad i \neq j.$$

Therefore,

$$Y = \bar{A}\ddot{Y} + BZ + (I - \bar{A})^{-1}V$$

$$E[\ddot{Y}, (I - \bar{A})^{-1}V] = E(\ddot{Y}, V^*) = 0, \text{ in spite of}$$
$$E(Y,V) = |\varepsilon| > 0$$

Q.E.D.

Corollary to theorem *1*: The least-squares bias (also called the Haavelmo bias) is so small that there is no definite empirical proof of the bias even if matrix (A) in the system (I) is a block form matrix under the condition of $E(Y,V) = |\varepsilon| > 0$. That is, the least-squares method can be applied to each relation in the system *sériatim*; however, there are no definite empirical proofs of the Haavelmo bias due to the inapplicability of controlled experimentation.

Unlike the theorem, the corollary thus has no theoretical proof; however, pragmatic arguments can be presented in favor of the corollary. In spite of the Haavelmo bias, the majority of empirical studies have been conducted using the single equation model. Their contributions have been too enormous to discount the corollary as a biased estimate. On the contrary, the corollary can serve as an enlightener for existing studies. The corollary acknowledges the Haavelmo bias but contends that it is possibly a marginal one, because the true interdependency is relatively less prevalent in structural models when compared with the affect of other problems, e.g., multicollinearity.[12]

Although the ID-school claims that the least-squares bias is more significant, for example, in macroeconomic models with annual data, the least-squares counterparts of the Klein-Goldberger equations are quite similar so that "it can be accounted for by the presence of sampling error."[13] The similarity also extend to the measurement of autocorrelation.

Accordingly, the corollary is extremely useful in a situation in which the construction of an ID-model is infeasible due to some difficulty, e.g., in a study of a demand, all structural equations, except the demand equation, cannot be specified or data for those equations are not available. A utilization of the corollary provides better logical accountability than the simple application of the least-squares method with apologetic reasons for the cost of estimation, availability of data, preliminary approximation, etc., for an estimation of an apparent ID-model.

Further arguments based on the corollary are presented after com-

[12]As was mentioned in Chapter III (B), multicollinearity appears in more accute form when we deal with the ID-system.

[13]L. R. Klein and A. S. Goldberger, *An Econometric Model of the United States, 1920–1952*, (Amsterdam: North-Holland Publishing Co., 1955), particularly p. 93.

pleting the main body of this comparative study.

REMARKS ON WOLD'S EO IPSO PREDICTOR[14]

The unbiased predictor (or stochastic relations defined in terms of conditional expectation) is newly termed as *eo ipso predictor* by Wold "on the consideration that the underlying notion of conditional expectation usually enters as an assumption, not as an implication," particularly for predictive models.

To paraphrase the above notion, it is useful to refer back to the development of the above section (B). The hypothetical relation,

$$Y = b_o + b_1X_1 + \ldots + b_nX_n + v$$

was specified in terms of conditional expectations, as the assumption:

$$E(Y/X_1,\ldots,X_n) = b_o + b_1X_1 + \ldots + b_nX_n,$$

which implies $E(v) = 0$; $E(v/X_i) = 0$; $E(v/X_i) = 0$, $(i = 1,2,\ldots,n)$ not as an implication. When the notion of this conditional expectation is extended for predictive purposes under *ceteris paribus* constraint, a prediction of a change in Y, in response to a change in X_i (any arbitrary combination of i), can be defined as *eo ipso* prediction. In symbols, we derive:

$$Y^p = E(Y/X_1 \rightarrow X_1 + \triangle_1,\ldots,X_n \rightarrow X_n + \triangle_n).$$

[14]These remarks are mainly summarized from Herman Wold's rigorous expositions. See his "Ends and Means in Econometric Model Building. Basic Considerations Reviewed," in Ulf Grenander (ed.), *Probability and Statistics* (New York: John Wiley & Sons, 1959), pp. 355–434; "A Generalization of Causal Chain Models," *Econometrica*, XXVIII (April, 1960), 443–463; "Construction Principles of Simultaneous Equations Models in Econometrics," *Bulletin de l'Institut International de Statistique*, XXXVIII, No. 4 (1961); "Unbiased Predictors," in J. Neyman (ed.), *Proceedings of the Fourth Berkeley Symposium on Mathematical Statistics and Probability*, Vol. I, (Berkeley: University of California Press, 1961), 719–761; "On the Consistency of Least-Squares Regression," *Sankhya*, Series A, XXV (1963), 211–215; and "The Approach of Model Building, Crossroads of Probability Theory, Statistics and Theory of Knowledge," in Herman Wold (sci. org.) *Model Building in the Human Sciences* (Monaco: Union Européene D'Editions, 1966), pp. 1–38.

Accordingly, the *eo ipso* predictor has a clear rationale for an experimental model in which the joint probability distribution is controlled by the experimenter's control. In the case of a non-experimental model, in spite of the fact that explanatory variables are ruled by the joint probability distribution which is not controllable, the model, depending on its purpose can be analogous to the controlled case in terms of the subject matter theory. Accordingly, because the conventional assumption of the residual terms are less rigorous, the assumption of the *eo ipso* predictor for a predictive model is more solidly founded as a basis for an investigation. Of course, a prediction of X_i must be done prior to that of Y, by some auxiliary device other than from the model.

Thus, an *eo ipso* predictor specification of a model is a very appropriate mechanism to identify a causal influence. It provides a theoretical and operational rationale for the method of least-squares regression in its structural form and for the reduced form of the CC-system. Moreover, the *eo ipso* predictor is unidirectional, in the sense of its irreversibility, but allows a chain of substitution processes.

To restate for clarity the above characteristic of unidirectionalism, let us postulate a stochastic model in which Y is causally influenced by X. This causal influence does not imply that the relations are isomorphic, i.e., mathematically equivalent. That is, even though

$$Y^p = E(Y/X_1,\ldots,X_n)$$
$$X^p \neq E(X_i/Y,X_j)$$

where i is arbitrary and $j = 1,\ldots,n$ excluding i. In general, this principle applies to any complicated situation, e.g., if Y is causally influenced by X and, in turn, X is causally influenced by Z, and so, then Y is causally influenced by Z via X and so on.

Thus, in retrospect, the main values of the predictive power of the behavioral relation is the conditional expectation of the structural form; and that the predictive power of each endogenous variable in the model to provide conditional expectations for the reduced form is derived from the chain substitution processes. However, note that in the ID-system, the substance or predictive power is only intensified in its form of reduced equations, allowing reversibility of a behavioral relation.

As a final remark, further investigation on this subject challenges one to raise his level of aspiration to the most difficult field, prediction. This challenge comes in the wake of the pioneering work done by Enders *A.* Robinson and Herman Wold who have proven that the *eo ipso* predictor is theoretically synonymous with the "minimum delay" in information theory and to the method of least-squares regression.[15] However, such a direction for this study is not only beyond the scope of this paper but beyond this author's intellectual capacity at this time.

Having studied theoretical and operational rationale of the CC-system in light of the causality assumption—causal influence as well as a flow of causation—in a system of simultaneous equations subject to disturbance terms, a technical classification of subsystems of the CC-system in line with the causal chain principle may be in order.

D. THE CLASSIFICATION OF THE CC-SYSTEM

Before the CC-system can be classified into subsystems, it may be necessary to restate briefly the causal chain principle. The causal chain principle is subject matter theory; information to employ causality assumptions in a system of stochastic, simultaneous equations is necessary before estimation technique can be initiated. The simplest form of the causal principle is the causal influence in each behavioral relation of a system. In turn, its generalized version becomes a flow of causation with links from variable-to-variable and relation-to-relation as in the arrow scheme of the system presented in Figure 4 in Chapter II.

1. **Vector Regression System**: A vector regression system is a very narrow and strict version of the causal chain principle. Each current endogenous variable is designed to be causally explained and predicted only by predetermined variables. This system is actually the same as Yule's autoregressive scheme except that the system is in a form of simultaneous equations together with the allowing for the other exogenous variables in the system.

In the system (I) above, if all the explanatory endogenous variables are assumed as zero a priori [or matrix $\bar{A}$ in (II) as zero a priori], the system (I) appears as a vector regression system. To put it another way, if $a_{ij} = 0$ in (I) or $\bar{A} = 0$ in (II) a priori, (II) can be written as:

---

[15]Enders A. Robinson and Herman Wold, "Minimum Delay Structure of Least-Squares/Eo Ipso Predicting Systems for Stationary Stochastic Processes, " M. Rosenblatt ed., *Time Series Analysis* (New York: John Wiley & Sons, 1963), pp. 192–196; also see Enders A. Robinson, "Wavelet Composition of Time Series, " *Econometric Model Building*, 37–106 and his "Recursive Decomposition of Stochastic Processes, " in *Ibid.*, 111–168.

$$Y = BZ + V.$$

Then each relation, as well as the system as a whole, can be specified as an explanatory or as an *eo ipso* predictor, i.e.,

$$Y^* = E(Y/Z) \text{ or}$$
$$Y^p = E(Y/Z \rightarrow Z + \triangle).$$

Figure 5.

Vector Regression System Explained by the Arrow Scheme

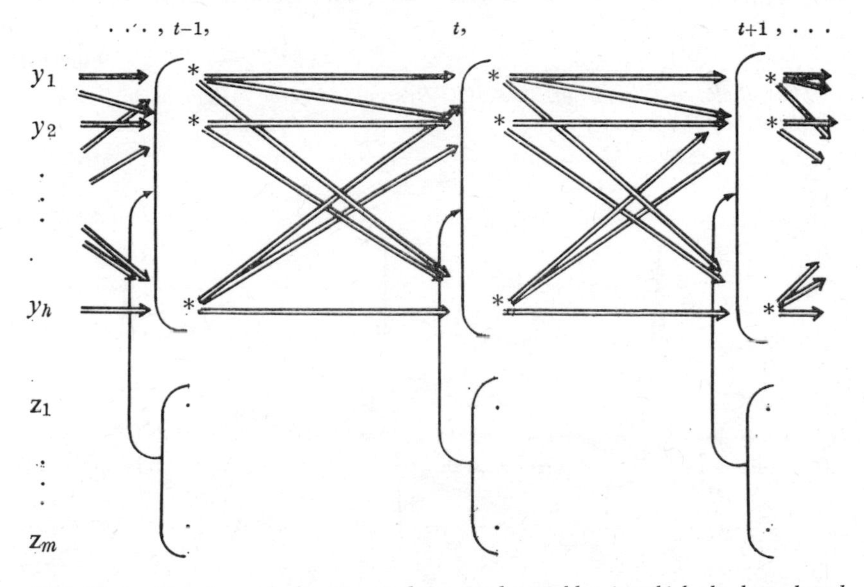

Note that z (i = 1,...,m) denotes predetermined variables in which the lagged and unlagged exogenous variables and the lagged endogenous variables are included. Cf. page 66 above.

Actually, the structural form (I) coincides with its reduced form (II). For example, the supply relation in the structural form in Chapter II (*B*):

$$S_t = a_1 P_{t-1} + b_1 Y_t + u_t,$$

is the behavioral relation of suppliers and, at the same time, is the reduced form of that relation, because it is practically assumed as $E(S_t/P_{t-1}, Y_t) = a_1 P_{t-1} + b_1 Y_t$.

Thus, in a vector regression system, no flow of causal influence among current endogenous variables exist and their variables are usually explained and predicted exclusively by their predetermined variables. As has been shown earlier, there is no doubt that for this system, the least-squares estimates are practically the same as those of the full-information maximum-likelihood method.

For reference, an arrow scheme diagram for the vector regression system is shown in Figure 5 above.

2. **Conventional CC-System**: This system has been demonstrated twice already in system (I) in section (*B*) above and in the illustrative hypothetical market model in Chapter II, (*B*). Consequently for understanding, it is adequate to mention that this system is a generalized version of the vector regression system under a constraint of a subdiagonal matrix of coeffici-

Figure 6.

The Reduced Form of the CC-System, Vector Regression Scheme, Explained by the Arrow Scheme

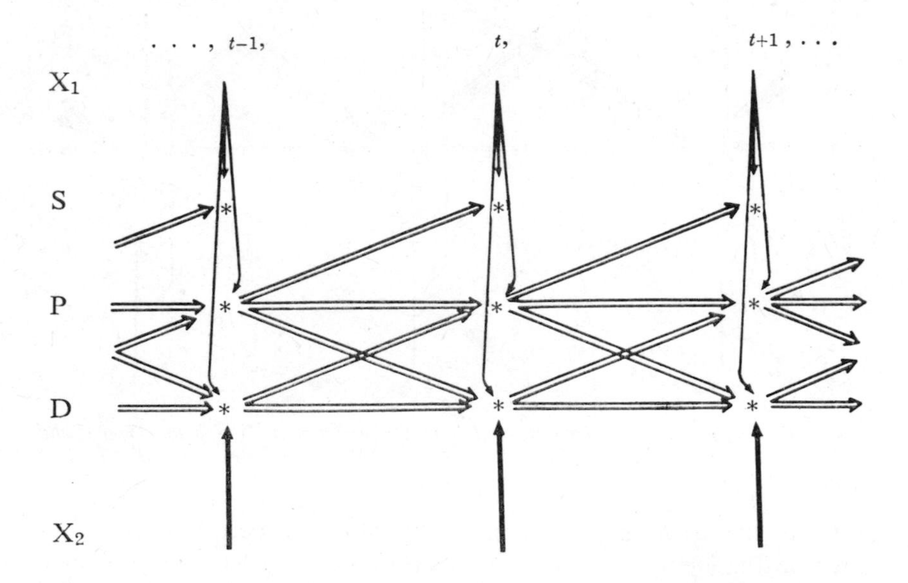

Compare with Figure 4, Chapter II (B), page 33, which is the structural form of the CC-system explained by the arrow scheme.

ents of explanatory endogenous variables. This generalized form (or the structural form) can be derived as a vector regression system (or the reduced form) through the chain substitution processes for expected values (or calculated values) or explained endogenous variables which follow the order in the subdiagonal matrix.

As to an arrow scheme diagram of the structural form, it is sufficient to point out Figure 4 in Chapter II, (*B*), rather than drawing a very complicated diagram with a large number of relations. When the chain substitution processes are completed, the arrow scheme diagram for the reduced form becomes the same as in Figure 5. For specific reference for analysis, it is better to draw the arrow scheme diagram of the reduced form of our hypothetical market model in Chapter II (*B*) as shown in Figure 6 above instead of a complicated multi-variable case, Figure 5.

In Figure 6, the non-zero elements in the subdiagonal matrix of (4a) in Chapter II (*B*)—i.e., the explanatory endogenous variables, S_t and P_t—are replaced by expected values in a specific sequence of iterative substitution (S_t and P_t or relations (3) and (2) order) in order to derive in Chapter II (B) the vector regression system (6a) which is described as the reduced form of the CC-system. Clearly, in Figure 6, there are no causal flows among the endogenous variables ($S_t \rightarrow P_t \rightarrow D_t$) unlike Figure 4 in Chapter I (*B*).

A more complete generalization without constraints on the subdiagonal matrix in a system is attempted in the following chapter.

CHAPTER V

CAUSALIZED INTERDEPENDENT SYSTEM

CHAPTER V

CAUSALIZED INTERDEPENDENT SYSTEM[1]

A causalized interdependent system (for brevity, CCID-system) may be defined as a system in which the substance of the interdependent (ID) system and the causal chain (CC) principle are connected in a system of simultaneous equations subject to disturbance terms. In this combined system, an indecomposable variety of matrices of coefficients of endogenous variables represents further generalization of the vector regression system. This generalization serves to implement an interdependency of economic variables while, at the same time, maintaining the causal chain principle to explain the causal relation between behaving units and an *eo ipso* predictor. The CCID-system, however, is not a synthesis of the ID- and CC-systems but is a hybrid, in the sense that it is only a partial adaptation of the two.

Although one can theoretically posit a causality in terms of a disequilibrium or dynamic model, one is obliged to recognize the reality of equilibrium or static assumptions. Therefore, in many cases, the imposition of a subdiagonal matrix of coefficients of explanatory endogenous variables

[1]This direction of the attempts to synthesize the two systems (the ID- and CC-systems) has been considered by Herman Wold. See his "Ends and Means in Econometric Model-Building. Basic Considerations Reviewed, " Ulf Grenander (ed.), *Probability and Statistics* (New York: John Wiley & Sons, 1959), pp. 355–434; "A Generalization of Causal Chain Models, " *Econometrica*, XXVIII (April, 1960), 443–463; and "Construction Principles of Simultaneous Equations Models in Econometrics, " *Bulletin de l'Institut International de Statitique,* XXXVIII (1962), 111–136.

on a system can lose its plausability. For example, in the case of a given manufacturer, the production unit and procurement unit must behave interdependently, as if they were a unified unit under constraint of a master plan by higher management. The two units plan together and take action according to their plan while checking each other to maintain equilibrium conditions. Notice, however, that this case does not involve causality which is only a valid assumption in a model between distinguished behaving units (autonomous units) that plan and act independently—at least during a certain time period—in accordance with their independent goals.

Obviously, cases of equilibrium need not be restricted to subdivisions of a behaving unit, as in the above case. Even between two or more economic units such as duopoly, whole units may act interdependently. At the same point in time and conditioned by each other, they may act as a single behaving unit through an explicit or tacit collusion. Another type of instantaneous equilibrium may occur in the activities of an auction or stock market.

Before proceeding further, some ideas about the concept of equilibrium, as it is applied in this study, should be made clear. The conventional expression of an equilibrium condition, (e.g., $D_t = S_t$, demand equals supply at time period t) in a model should not be mistaken for an identity. Observationally and conceptually, demand and supply have different meanings for different economic units—consumers and producers whose goals are basically independent and different. For example, according to Klappholz and Mishan:

> . . . no hypothesis whatever about equilibrium conditions can be inferred from identities.
>
> . . . we have not been opposing the use of "tautologies" in the sense of inference in economics. . . . Nor have we any quarrel with the formulation of identities as such.
>
> . . .
>
> . . . they may help us to organize our thinking or to expose logical errors . . . however, it is the practice of and the arguments for, the substitution in economic models of equations which are identities, when, in fact, the empirical implications which economists purport to deduce from these models follow only if such equations are not identities but genuinely independent equations—equations that are, in effect, independent empirical statements.[2]

[2]K. Klappholz and E. J. Mishan, "Identities in Economic Models," *Economica*, XXIX (May, 1962), 126. The similar arguments are presented by Harold Dickson in his "Logical Aspects of Identities in Mathematics and in Economics," *Kyklos*, XIII (1960), 261–272.

In this chapter, the hybrid CCID-system is developed. This combined use of the ID- and CC-systems is deemed necessary if interdependency and causality are to co-exist in a system. Careful attention is given to the elimination of the dilemmas found in the ID-system so that improved theoretical interpretation and operational use of an ideal system can be established. A structural form of the ID-system is designed in terms of conditional expectations and of an *eo ipso* predictor rather than emphasis on a reduced form. To paraphrase the above, the structural form of the CCID-system plays a main role in the new model, unlike the reduced form which plays an almost exclusive role in the ID-system. Note that, at least in theory, both the structural form and the reduced form play equivalent roles in the CC-system as isomorphism.

Although the CCID-system is a further generalization of the vector regression system discussed in the previous chapter—in which the system included a block matrix of coefficients of endogenous variables—the vector regression system can be further subclassified in three ways in accordance with the flow of causation or the direction of an arrow scheme. These subsystems are the bicausal-chain system, the circular-chain system, and the interdependent system. (Technically, the ID-system is an extreme version of a generalized vector regression system expressed by the direction of an arrow scheme.)

In the following section (A), these three subsystems are theoretically developed in the order: bicausal-chain system, circular-chain system, and ID-system. In section (B) these subsystems are compared in terms of an operational rationale.

A. SUBSYSTEMS OF THE CCID-SYSTEM

The simplified interdependent market model in Chapter II (A), *the ID-system*,

$$S_t = a_1 P_t + b_1 X_{1t} + u_{1t} \tag{1}$$

$$D_t = a_2 P_t + b_2 X_{2t} + u_{2t} \tag{2}$$

$$S_t = D_t = Q_t \tag{3}$$

is employed again for convenience, because the CCID-system is identical to the ID-system in its formality. However the former is designed to furnish an economic operational interpretation by the flow of causation in a system. A key difference of the ID-system may arise due to its subject matter theory which guides the arrow scheme specification of the system. In addition, this arrow scheme specification may suggest assumptions for the model, particularly for the specification of residual terms and other variables rather than the other way around.

In specific, the following three sets of illustrative figures for the model below—demonstrating the arrow scheme of the bicausal-chain, circular-chain, and ID-systems—contain for comparative purposes the same assumptions for supply and demand relations. Other assumptions are: instantaneous equilibrium, conventional normality and independence of disturbance terms, non-autocorrelation, and absence of measurement errors in the variables. Also, notational meanings remain the same as in Chapter II (A) as does the measurement of variables as deviations from their mean values.

1. The Bicausal-Chain System.—The bicausal-chain system is simply an

Figure 7.

The Bicausal-Chain Arrow Scheme Specification of the Interdependent Model where $Q = D = S$

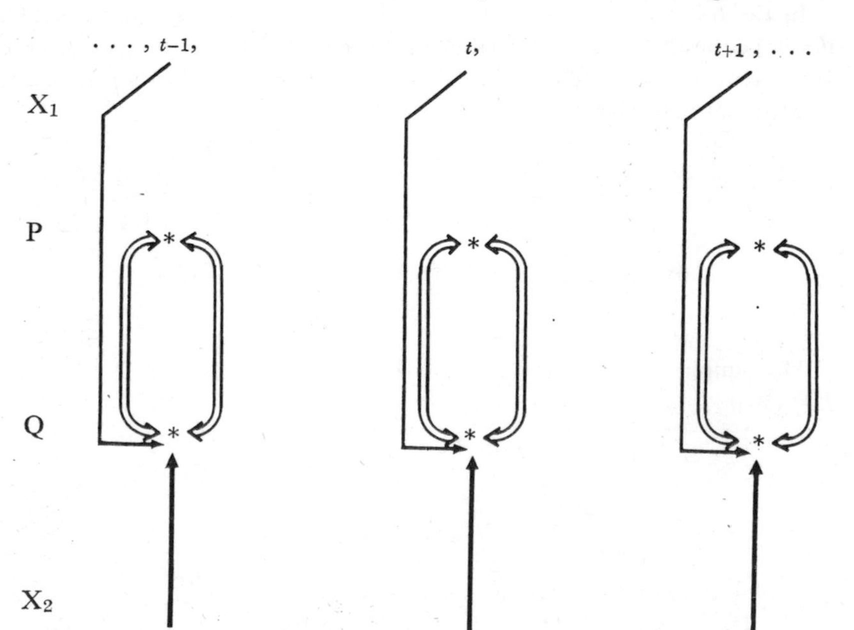

ID-system but with a bicausalized specification of a structural model and constructed in accordance with a priori subject matter theory.

Taking the above three equations, (1)–(3), of the ID-system, one can specify the bicausal-chain system in terms of causal interpretation. As such the ID-system can be respecified in more detail than was done in line with causality, by which the model has been described as a mutual interdependence of economic variables when equilibrium assumptions are implemented.

The bicausal-chain specification can be constructed simply as in Figure 7 above. In Figure 7, the double line arrow indicates a direction of causal influence from the explanatory endogenous variable to the explained endogenous variables; and the single line arrow indicates causal influence by the exogenous variables. Specifically, the quantity (S_t) supplied at time t is causally explained by the price (P_t) at time t, as well as the exogenous variable (X_{1t}) at time t; the quantity demanded (D_t) at t is causally explained by the P_t as well as X_{2t}. Of course, the constraint is $S_t = D_t = Q_t$, as the assumption of instantaneous equilibrium.

In spite of identical appearance to the original model, the bicausal-chain specification should be considered in detail. The following complete specification of the model, in terms of conditional expectations, is a logical preliminary before analyzing the model.

(4) $$E(Q/P,X_1) = a_1P + b_1X_1$$

(5) $$E(Q/P,X_2) = a_1P + b_2X_2$$

(Time subscript t is not and will not be written for convenience.)

where $E(P,u_1) = E(P,u_2) = 0 = E(u_1) = E(u_2)$ are implied.

This author's theorem and corollary in the previous chapter are applicable here for theoretical justification of the model. Simply, $E(P,u_1) = E(P,u_2) = 0$ is justifiable, if u_1 and u_2 are not large or $E(P,u_1) = \varepsilon$ and $E(P,u_2) = \varepsilon'$, where ε and ε' are arbitrary small constants. For example, if a public authority controls the price of goods, or a monopolist fixes the price. Then, the method of least-squares regression can be applied to the structural form *sériatim*.

The reduced form of the system is:

(6) $$P = m_1X_1 + m_2X_2 + m_3(u_2 - u_1)$$

(7) $$Q = m_4X_1 + m_5X_2 + m_6(a_1u_2 - a_2u_1)$$

where $m_1 = -b_1/(a_1 - a_2)$ $m_2 = b_2/(a_1 - a_2)$ $m_3 = 1/(a_1 - a_2)$

$m_4 = -a_2b_1/(a_1 - a_2)$ $m_5 = a_1b_2/(a_1 - a_2)$ $m_6 = m_3$.

Because the structural from (1)–(3) is respecified as (4)–(5) under conditional expectations, the reduced form (6)–(7) cannot be specified in terms of conditional expectations[3] or an *eo ipso* predictor. That is,

$$(8) \qquad E(P/X_1,X_2) \neq m_1X_1 + m_2X_2$$

$$(9) \qquad E(Q/X_1,X_2) \neq m_4X_1 + m_5X_2$$

where these specifications imply

$$E[P,m_3(u_2 - u_1)] \neq 0 \neq E[Q,m_6(a_1u_2 - a_2u_1)].$$

Actually, (8) and (9) are the sequel of (4) and (5), in general.

Therefore, the reduced form (6) and (7) cannot be estimated by the method of least-squares regression, and the structural form of the ID-system cannot be estimated *sériatim* by the least-squares regression method, due to (8) and (9). However, it is possible to transform the parameters of the structural form into the reduced form in the system, and to transform the parameters of the reduced form into the structural form in the ID-system. In the example, a simple transformation can be performed on this model due to its identifiability.

2. The Circular-Chain System.—The circular-chain system is also simply an ID-system in its formal appearance, but with a circular-chain specification of the structural model with a priori information.

For brevity of explanation, the relations of the three subsystems are taken again as an example. When the ID-system is respecified in accordance with a circular-causality assumption, rather than a straightforward mutual dependency of economic variables, the result is the below arrow scheme diagram, Figure 8. All notational and figurative meanings remain the same as in Figure 7.

The causal explanation of Figure 10 has a similar foundation of logical explanation as the bicausal-chain system. The difference is only the direction of the arrows as shown in the figure in which Q is causally influenced by P and X_1; P is causally influenced by Q and X_2 under the equilibrium assumption.

Specifying the model as prescribed by the direction of the arrows,

$$(1) \qquad Q_t = a_1P_t + b_1X_{1t} + u_{1t}$$

$$(2) \qquad P_t = a_2Q_t + b_2X_{2t} + u_{2t}$$

$$(3) \qquad S_t = D_t = Q_t$$

the positions of P_t and Q_t in relation (2) are interchanged while the rest

[3] For the reason, see Chapter III (B) above.

Figure 8.
The Circular-Chain Arrow Scheme Specification of the Interdependent Model Where $Q = D = S$

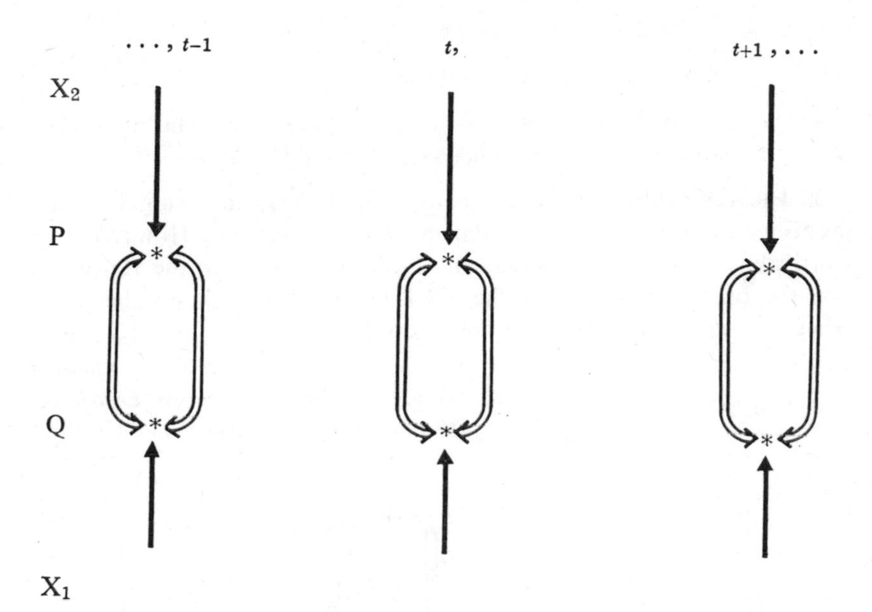

remain the same as before. Accordingly, following the arrows, the system can be specified in terms of conditional expectations (the time subscript t will not be shown below for convenience):

(4) $$E(Q/P,X_1) = a_1P + b_1X_1$$

(5) $$E(P/Q,X_2) = a_2Q + b_2X_2$$

Therefore, application of the least-square regression method is rationalized for estimation of the parameters of the system *sériatim*.

As a result, the reduced form cannot be specified in terms of conditional expectations and hence the form cannot be estimated by thel east-squares method as in the bicausal-chain system, in general. However, a derivation of the parameters of the reduced form from the structural form is possible, depending upon the identifiability of the system.

The reduced form becomes:

(6) $$P = m_1X_1 + m_2X_2 + m_3(a_2u_1 + u_2)$$

$$(7) \qquad Q = m_4X_1 + m_5X_2 + m_6(a_1u_2 + u_1)$$

where $m_1 = b_1a_2/(1 - a_1a_2)$ $m_2 = b_2/(1 - a_1b_1)$ $m_3 = 1/(a_1 - a_2)$

$$m_4 = b_1/(1 - a_1a_2) \quad m_5 = a_1b_2/(1 - a_1a_2) \quad m_6 = m_3$$

$$(8) \qquad E(P/X_1,X_2) \neq m_1X_1 + m_2X_2$$

$$(9) \qquad E(Q/X_1,X_2) \neq m_4X_1 + m_5X_2.$$

(8) and (9) clearly demonstrate why the least-squares method is not rational for the estimation of the parameters of (6) and (7) *sériatim.*

3. The ID-system.—As was explained previously in detail, it is not necessary to specify the ID-system in an arrow scheme. However, it is worthwhile to visualize a fundamental difference between the ID-system and the other subsystems of the CCID-system, in light of the arrow scheme diagram as is shown in the below Figure 9.

Figure 9.

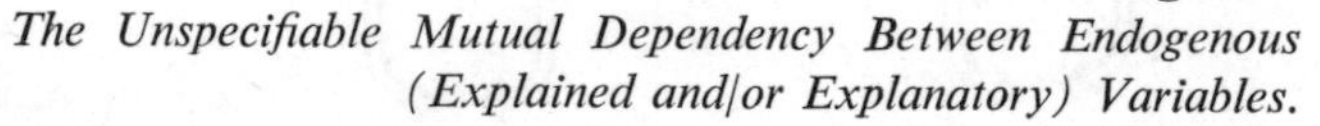

The Unspecifiable Mutual Dependency Between Endogenous (Explained and/or Explanatory) Variables.

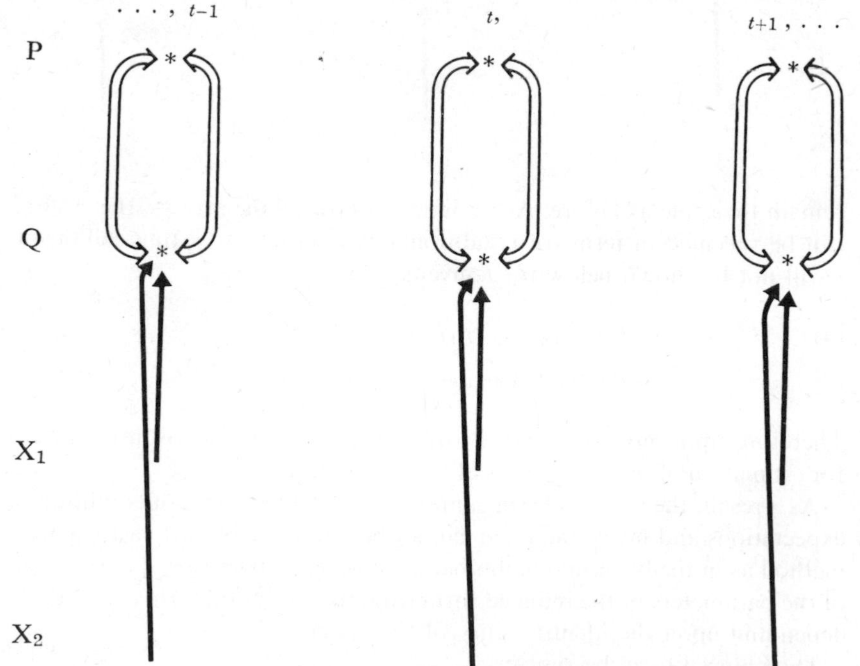

The explanation of Figure 9 has the same foundation as in the earlier two figures, 7 and 8. In Figure 9, however, the double line arrows indicate that the endogenous variables (explained or explanatory without any discrimination) are unspecifiably and mutually dependent on each other. This precise mutual dependency between economic variables is the most extreme version of generalization of the vector regression system and there is no way to rationalize the system in light of a causal influence, except in the sense of causal influence. There seems to be no "flow" concept at all.

In accordance with Figure 9, the system appears to be formally the same as the bicausal-chain system.

$$S_t = a_1P_t + b_1X_{1t} + u_{1t} \tag{1}$$

$$D_t = a_2P_t + b_2X_{2t} + u_{2t} \tag{2}$$

$$S_t = D_t = Q_t \tag{3}$$

(Time subscript t will not be shown below for convenience.)

Due to the instantaneous mutual interdependency of the two endogenous variables, Q and P, it is impossible to describe the model in terms of conditional expectations or to give any causal influence assumption; symbolically,

$$E(Q/P,X_1) \neq a_1P + b_1X_1 \tag{4}$$

$$E(Q/P,X_2) \neq a_2P + b_2X_2 \tag{5}$$

Therefore, the least-squares regression method should not be applied to the structural form *sériatim*.

On the other hand, the reduced form,

$$P = m_1X_1 + m_2X_2 + m_3(u_2 - u_1) \tag{6}$$

$$Q = m_4X_1 + m_5X_2 + m_6(a_1u_2 - a_2u_1) \tag{7}$$

where $m_1 = - b_1/(a_1 - a_2)$ $m_2 = b_2/(a_1 - a_2)$ $m_3 = 1/(a_1 - a_2)$

$m_4 = - a_2b_1(a_1 - a_2)$ $m_5 = a_1b_2/(a_1 - a_2)$ $m_6 = m_3$

can be estimated by the method of least-squares regression *sériatim*, because (6) and (7) can be specified as,

$$E(P/X_1,X_2) = m_1X_1 + m_2X_2 \tag{8}$$

$$E(Q/X_1,X_2) = m_4X_1 + m_5X_2. \tag{9}$$

Thus far the essential differences among the subsystems of the generalized version of the vector regression system have been demonstrated on operational grounds. Also on the systemic level of comparison, several divergencies occur among the ID-, CC-, and CCID-systems. First in the ID-system, operations proceed from reduced forms; the CCID-system operates with structural forms. In the former, the structural parameters are transformed from the reduced form; in the latter, the reduced form parameters are transformed from the structural form. Consequently, as was argued in Chapter III (B), the former fails in the dilemma of interpreting the coefficients of the behavioral relations; whereas, the latter fails in the dilemma of interpreting the coefficients of the non-autonomous reduced form. This relative superiority of the ID- and CCID-systems depends upon the purpose of model-building; however, in this author's opinion, the dilemma of the CCID-system is less serious than that of the ID-system, because the main interest of model-building more frequently focuses on the coefficients of and predictions by the behavioral relations of an economic unit rather than on a prediction of economic variables. Second, unlike the ID-system, the CCID-system does not project a specification error of one relation or of one variable onto the whole network of a model, unless a prediction of explanatory endogenous variables from the reduced form is necessary.[4] Third, the CCID-system is not troubled with problems of identification and with possible accumulation of multicollinearity and autocorrelation as in the ID-system, as long as the main interest focuses on behavior relations. Finally, a chance of specification error inherent in the CC-system, due to a limitation of the subdiagonal matrix of the system, does not occur in the CCID-system.

In retrospect, the CCID-system has several advantages over both the CC- and ID-systems in simultaneous equation model-building. The CCID-system, in light of the "flow" concept, however, is less dynamic than the CC-system but is more dynamic than the ID-system. Of special note is the conclusion that the CC-system does not have the dilemma found in the other systems.

Furthermore, in the illustrative figures, 7–9, the property of interdependency is explicitly implemented by the instantaneous equilibrium assumption—in Figure 7, Q is causally explained by P, X_1 and P, X_2 respectively; in Figure 8, the value of one variable is causally explained by the values of other variables which must be sequentially determined in accordance with a flow of causation; and in Figure 9, values of P and Q can be explained by X_1 and X_2, respectively, due to the rigid mutual dependency between P and Q and without having to explain the path of

---

[4]Cf. A wrong conjecture of the CC-system is mentioned by E. Malinvaud in his *Statistical Methods of Econometrics* (Chicago: Rand McNally & Co., 1966), p. 543.

equilibrating forces.

In order to conduct further comparative analysis of the ID-system and CCID-system, it is necessary to translate the above development into other theoretical and operational frameworks.

B. A THEORETICAL AND OPERATIONAL COMPARISON OF THE ID-SYSTEM AND THE CCID-SYSTEM (BICAUSAL-CHAIN AND CIRCULAR-CHAIN SUB-SYSTEMS)

Although the three systems, in general, may generate three different stationary stochastic processes, it may be equally reasonable to assume that one process can incorporate the three different processes. That is, the three models can be designed to generate the same stationary stochastic process. In this case, there is no way of knowing which one of the processes is responsible for generating the result when a realization has been generated from any of these three models.

Taking again the example given for the ID-system in (1)–(3) above, the three subsystems will be scrutinized to obtain a single result. Here the one-time lag of the price variable (P_{t-1}) is employed in the place of P_t in the supply relation (1) and the exogenous variables, X_{1t} and X_{2t}, are disregarded for the sake of simplicity, viz,

$$S_t = a_1 P_{t-1} + u_{1t} \quad (1)$$

$$D_t = a_2 P_t + u_{2t} \quad (2)$$

$$S_t = D_t = Q_t \quad (3)$$

The simplest cobweb model of supply-and-demand market relations under instantaneous equilibrium is established for the three subsystems from which the same stationary stochastic processes are generated. (Of course, the positions of D_t and P_t in (2) are interchanged for the circular-chain system.) For the stated purpose, it is necessary to assume that the three stationary stochastic processes from the three subsystems are mutually equal with respect to the first and second order moments of stationary and Gauss-Markoff processes.[5]

[5]The Gauss-Markoff process type denotes that all joint probability distributions for

As a consequence of two dimensional stochastic variables, the processes are:

$$\ldots,(P_{t-2}, Q_{t-2}), (P_{t-1}, Q_{t-1}), (P_t, Q_t), (P_{t+1}, Q_{t+2}),\ldots$$

$$(1) \qquad E(P_t) = E(Q_t) = 0$$

$$(2) \qquad E(P_t^2) = E(Q_t^2) = 1$$

$$(3) \qquad E(Q_t, P_t) = -a_2$$

$$(4) \qquad E(P_{t-1}, Q_t) = a_1$$

$$(5) \qquad E(P_{t-1}, P_t) = -\varrho \qquad t = 0, \pm 1, \pm 2,\ldots$$

where (1) and (2) standardize the variables; P_t and Q_t are to be observed as deviations from their means, with the standard deviations as measuring units.

Because the processes have five covariances, (2)–(5), with zero or one-time lag (i.e., $t = 0, -1$), remaining as covariances, $E(Q_{t-1},P_t)$ and $E(Q_{t-1},Q_t)$, they become functions of the unspecified parameter $-\varrho$. Namely, the remaining product moments are determined from the character of the model, as in Figure 10 below.

In this figure, since (2) implies that the covariances are correlation coefficients, the three unspecified parameters, [$-\varrho$ and the functions of $-\varrho$, viz, $E(Q_{t-1},Q_t)$ and $E(Q_{t-1},P_t)$], are subject to the following restrictions:

$$(5a) \qquad -1 \leq E(P_{t-1}, P_t) = -\varrho \text{ where } -\varrho \leq 1$$

$$(6) \qquad -1 \leq E(Q_{t-1}, Q_t) \leq 1$$

$$(7) \qquad -1 \leq E(Q_{t-1}, P_t) \leq 1$$

The three cobweb-types of structural forms are constructed below with the above nine parameters in order to differ only in the coefficients of P_t (i.e., a_2) in the demand relation of each model; each supply relation in the three models is non-controversial, because the relation coincides in their

---

the variables are normal, and the conditional distribution for one or more variables at time period t, knowing the development of the process up to and including a period $_{t-1}$, coincides with the conditional distribution when only the variables at period $_{t-1}$ are known.

A stochastic process $\{y_t\}$ is called a Gauss-Markoff process if $E(y_t/y_{t-1}, y_{t-2},\ldots, y_{t-i}) = E(y_t/y_{t-1})$ for all $i = 2,3,\ldots.$

Therefore the following autoregressive process $y_t + b_1 y_{t-1} + \ldots + b_i y_{t-i} = u_t$, $-\infty < t < \infty$ is a Gauss-Markoff process if and only if $i = 1$.

reduced forms where $E(P_{t-1},u_{1t}) = 0 = E(P_{t-1},u_{2t})$, for all three models.

I. The ID-System

(1) $$S_t = a_1 P_{t-1} + u_{1t}$$

(2) $$D_t = (a_1/\varrho) P_t + u_{2t}$$

Figure 10.

The Five Fundamental Covariances and the Remaining Unspecified Covariances in Stationary and Gauss-Markoff Processes of (P_t,Q_t) with $t = 0, \pm 1, \pm 2, \ldots$

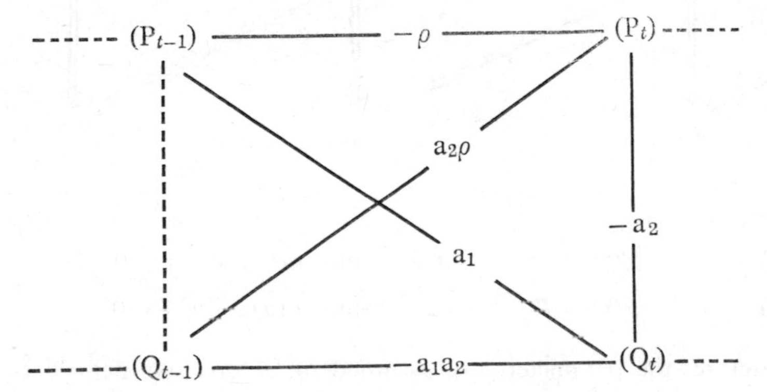

Since the main significance of the ID-system is its utilization of the reduced form of equations, theoretical coefficient of P_t in (2) can be derived through $P_t = f(P_{t-1},u_{1t},u_{2t})$ as in (6) below. Specifications by conditional expectation is;

(3) $$E(Q_t/P_{t-1}) = a_1 P_{t-1}$$

(4) $$E(Q_t/P_t) \neq (-a_1/\varrho) P_t$$

The reduced form

(5) same as (1)

(6) $$P_t = -\varrho P_{t-1} + \varrho/(a_1 u_{2t} - a_1 u_{1t})$$

with

(7) same as (3)

(8) $$E(P_t/P_{t-1}) = -\varrho P_{t-1}$$

and

(9) $$E(u_{2t}, u_{2,t\pm1}) = E(u_{1t},u_{1,t\pm i}) = E(u_{2t},u_{1,t\pm i}) = 0$$

$$i = 1,2,\ldots$$

The arrow scheme of the structural form (1)–(2) under the instantaneous equilibrium assumption can be shown as,

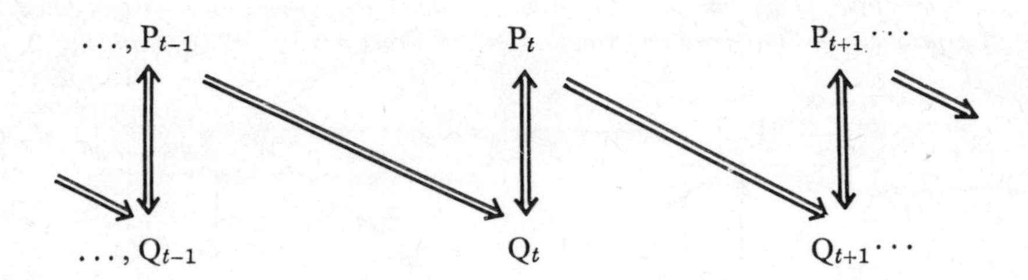

(10) $E(Q,Q_{t-1}) = -\ a_1a_2$ since $E(u_{2,t-1},u_{1t}) = 0$

(11) $E(Q_{t-1},P_t) = a_2$ since $E(u_{2,t-1},u_{2t}) = 0$

Therefore, the parameters are assumed to be precisely defined by this ID-system, even if arrows between P and Q are not uni-directional.

II. The Bicausal-Chain System

(1) Same as (1) in I above

(2) $D_t = -\ a_2P_t + u_{2t}$

with

(3) Same as (3) in I

(4) $E(Q_t/P_t) = -\ a_2P_t$

The reduced form:

(5) Same as (5) in I

(6) $P = (-a_1/a_2)P_{t-1} + 1/a_2(u_{2t} - u_1)$

with

(7) Same as (7) in I

(8) $E(P_t/P_{t-1}) \neq (-a_1/a_2)P_{t-1}$

and

(9) Same as (9) in I except the last term,

$$E(u_{2t}, u_{1}, t \pm i) = 0, \text{ i.e., } E(u_{2t}, u_{1,t-1}) \neq 0$$

The arrow scheme of the structural form can be shown as

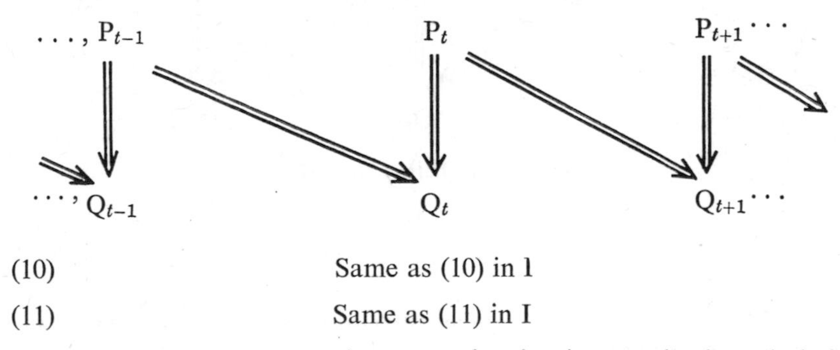

(10) Same as (10) in I

(11) Same as (11) in I

Again the parameters can be assumed to be circumscribed precisely by the bicausal-chain system. However, each arrow is uni-directional, thus distinctively indicating a causal influence, unlike in I.

III. The Circular-Chain System

(1) Same as (1) in I and II above.

(2) $P_t = - a_2 Q_t + u_{2t}$

with

(3) Same as (3) in I and II.

(4) $E(P_t/Q_t) = - a_2 Q_t$

The reduced form

(5) Same as (5) in I and II.

(6) $P_t = - a_1 a_2 P_{t-1} + (u_{2t} - a_2 u_{1t})$

with

(7) Same as (7) in I and II.

(8) $E(P_t/P_{t-1}) \neq - a_1 a_2 P_{t-1}$

and

(9) Same as (9) in II.

The arrow scheme of the structural form can be shown as

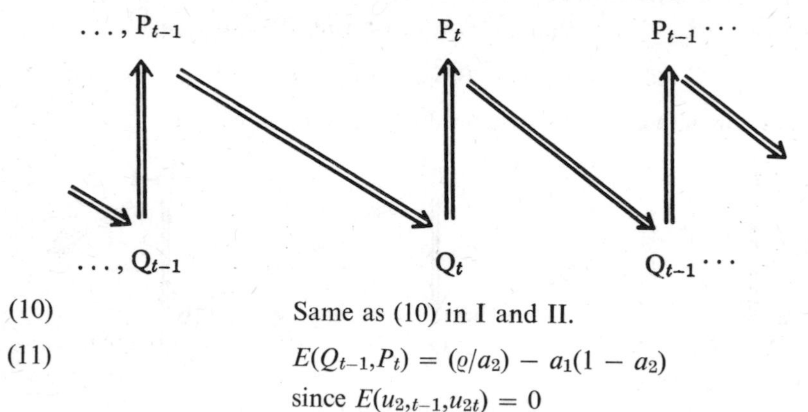

(10) Same as (10) in I and II.

(11) $E(Q_{t-1},P_t) = (\varrho/a_2) - a_1(1 - a_2)$
since $E(u_{2,t-1},u_{2t}) = 0$

Thus each arrow is uni-directional indicating a causal influence as in II, but the direction of influence is reversed, i.e., from Q to P.

The nine parameters have produced identical stationary Markoff processes. Therefore, it is not possible to know which time series data are generated from which system among the three subsystems. However, $E(u_{1,t-1},u_{2t}) = 0$ in (9) holds only for the ID-system. $E(u_{1,t-1},u_{2t}) = 0$ does not imply a zero correlation between the disturbance terms in each equation and the other variables on the right-hand side of the same equation. In other words, the idea that the disturbance terms of the structural forms are uncorrelated is not identical with the assumption of zero correlation between the disturbance terms, i.e., the disturbance terms are non-autocorrelated and are uncorrelated with the lagged variables.

Specifically, what has been demonstrated is the fact that the model can be distinguished as I, II, or III, only if the flow of causation is specified by an arrow scheme. The structural forms of the CCID-system—bicausal-chain and circular-chain—should be specified in terms of conditional expectations or an *eo ipso* predictor which depends upon the causal chain principle. Then, the rationale of the method of least-squares regression becomes a non-controversial matter, particularly when the method is supported by the theorem and corollary in the previous chapter, i.e., the rationality of $E(P_t,u_{2t}) = 0$ in the bicausal-chain system and $E(Q_t,u_{2t}) = 0$ in the circular-chain system.

In the ID-system, the least-squares method includes biases, in general, due to the unspecified parameter ϱ. In other words, the biases are a logical consequence of nonspecifiability of the structural form as conditional expectations, i.e., relations (4)–(5) in section A above. However the reduced form of the ID-system can be specified in terms of conditional expectations and an *eo ipso* predictor.

Therefore, the CCID-system is distinctively different from the ID-system in the development of the structural form or the reduced form, in spite of their similar appearances. The CCID-system's operative use of the structural form is more similar to the CC-system than to the ID-system. The ID-system utilizes the structural form as a theoretical tool to derive the reduced form in prediction. Consequently, the ID-system has a dilemma in the explicit use of the structural form; whereas, the CCID-system has a dilemma in the explicit use of the reduced form. This difference exists because of the stochastic non-equivalence between the structural form and the reduced form in the two systems. As was mentioned, the parameters of the structural form may be derived from the reduced form in the ID-system and those of the reduced form may be derived from the structural form in the CCID-system. However, they meet an analogous dilemma in attempts to explain and predict the behavior of economic units in the ID-system and of those dilemmas in the reduced form of the CCID-system.

On the other hand, the CC-system exhibits none of these dilemmas of the ID- and CCID-systems. The CC-system, however, is limited in its usefulness in the construction of an empirical model due to the inflexibility of subdiagonal matrices and to the construction arising from subject matter theory or information. Furthermore, once the CC-system is constructed without a clearcut subject matter theory, some of its relations do not make sense in actual operation due to its rigid assumptions. The ID-system has other ways of fragility since misspecification of one relation can be transmitted throughout the whole network of the vector regression scheme—the reduced form. The case is true for the CCID-system in reverse order.

Certainly, it may be true, as in the ID-system, that various kinds of "relations" can be defined as the properties of the joint probability law if a model is assumed to be an indirect specification of the joint probability law of observed economic variables. However, stochastic simultaneous equation model-building is much more than an interpretation of joint probability. For instance, an asymmetric or directed (causal) relation in economic theory, as well as in economic policy, cannot be satisfied by non-specific "relation." Specified ways of "relation" are necessitated.

Pragmatically, when a model is going to be constructed for empirical testing, no matter what kind of model it may be, the causal concepts for each and every relation are considered as the backbone of the model in light of the subject matter information of the model builder.

CHAPTER VI

A CASE STUDY OF THE INTERDEPENDENT, CAUSAL CHAIN, AND CAUSALIZED INTERDEPENDENT SYSTEMS

— A U.S. TIN-CAN INDUSTRY, 1950-1967

CHAPTER VI

A CASE STUDY OF THE INTERDEPENDENT, CAUSAL CHAIN, AND CAUSALIZED INTERDEPENDENT SYSTEMS —A U.S. TIN-CAN INDUSTRY, 1950-1967

In previous chapters the several methods of structural model-building have been compared and discussed in terms of economic theory, statistics, and probability theory in stationary time series. The interdependent (ID) system and the causal chain (CC) system have been discussed in detail on a comparative basis, and the causalized interdependent (CCID) system which contains bicausal chain and circular chain systems has been introduced as a hybrid of the latter two systems.

In the course of the discussion, each system, at least in its formal appearance, has been considered as a generalized version of the vector regression system. The differences in generalization among the systems have appeared to be a matter of a degree not in kind, ranging from moderate to extreme cases. These four systems, however, have both merits and demerits in describing systemic behavior. From theoretical arguments, it has been shown that the CC-system has relative superiority over the other systems, in light of the "flow" concept, regardless of its inflexibility for a wider application.

It is the main task of this chapter to compare the four approaches of structural model-building with their empirical results, employing actual time series data of the tin-can industry for the years 1950–1966, inclusive.

The four models are constructed as similarly as possible in order to provide an unbiased basis for comparison; otherwise, these models would differ to a certain degree, if a model were constructed for the study of the tin-can industry per se without any constraints for comparative study.

Subsequently, it is not this author's purpose to derive a definite final judgement on the superior performance of any one system. Furthermore, direct references to real models for the evaluation of empirical results of the theoretical models are for the most part unavailable to this author's knowledge. Relatively few econometric studies have been done on producers' goods like tin-cans, particularly for studies employing a system of simultaneous equations.

On the other hand, it is hoped that "two birds can be killed with one stone. " The first aim is the building and testing of alternative models for the tin-can industry in order to fulfill the main purpose of this chapter —a comparison of the four systems with their empirical results, in accordance with the theoretical developments of the preceding chapters. The second aim is to shed light on this author's future research for more comprehensive construction methods for a tin-can industry model.[1] These simple and similar models will be constructed to play roles as exploratory models for the tin-can industry. A well-performing empirical model does not necessarily demand a complicated one.

In section A below, the background of the tin-can industry is described in light of its historical activities and of theoretical discussions developed prior to the construction of models. After constructing the models, empirical coefficients of each system are calculated and compared in accordance with the above developemnts.

A. BACKGROUND OF THE U.S. TIN-CAN INDUSTRY

1. History

From a relatively insignificant industry, the tin-can industry, at the

---

[1]A research fellowship from the State University of New York Research Foundation has been granted for my proposal, "An Econometric Model of the U.S. Tin-Can Industry, " for the Summer of 1969.

turn of this century, has developed into one of the more important industries in the U.S. economy. "Packaging in all its forms is an integral part of modern mass production . . . the (present day) tin-can industry is by far the biggest supplier of rigid packages in the nations. "[2]

Early in its development, the American Can Company successfully monopolized the industry during the Great Merger Movement. American Can combined with more than 100 other producers and by 1903 its seller concentration ratio was more than 90 percent.[3] American Can's excess profit, together with a rapidly growing demand, brought entry of the Continental Can Company into the industry in 1904. The U.S. v. American Can Company case of 1916 indicated duopoly competition between these two rivals.[4] By 1939, the two leading companies' seller concentration ratio was near 80 percent and the rest of the shipments of the industry were divided among almost 100 independent companies.

Since World War II, the duopoly condition between the two giants has continued. In 1963, the six largest tin-can companies, among almost 100 firms, sold over 80 percent of the total sales (excluding captive cans) and the two giants sold a little less than 70 percent of the total sales. The next four leading companies are National Can, Crown Can, Heekin Can, and Hoffman Machinery, none of which accounted for more than six percent of the value of shipments.

Although the two giants' seller concentration ratio has apparently decreased gradually, this simple arithmetic ratio underestimates the true strength of their power. In other words, decline in the ratio does not represent decline in control of the industry by the big two.[5] Despite a tremendous growth of physical size and operational scale of the two giants, major reasons for the decreasing arithmetic ratio can be found.

First, tin-cans for canning industries in isolated areas can be easily

---

[2]Charles H. Hession, "The Metal Container Industry, " Walter Adams (ed.), *The Structure of American Industry* 3rd ed. (New York: the Macmillan Co., 1961), p. 430. Words in parenthesis are mine.

[3]United States v. American Can Company, 230 Fed. 859 (1916).

[4]*Ibid.*

[5]For example, from 1955 to 1956, Continental Can's assets rose from $382 million to $666 million. In addition, Continental Can's sales share in the beer-can market was already 43 percent of the total market in 1955 and 46 percent in 1957. Demand for beer-cans is highly seasonal but it makes higher profits than other cans.

Furthermore, Continental Can was the 36th largest manufacturing company in 1962 and the 40th in 1963; and ACC was the 38th in 1962 and the 41st in 1963. There is not much difference in their largeness by any other criteria, such as assets and number of employees. See U.S. v. Continental Can Company, *et al.*, 84 S. Ct. 1738 (No. 369), 1964 and U.S. Congress, Senate, Subcommittee on Antitrust and Monopoly, *Hearings, Economic Concentration,* Pt. I. pp. 281–282 and 401–421.

supplied by small scale independent tin-can producers within the area without experiencing coersive pressure from the giants who are not willing to meet the demands. Second, a variety of speciality cans, whose demand has grown, are not adequate products for the larger economies of scale production. Third, tin-cans are relatively cheap containers but they are bulky, giving some transport-cost-shelter to regional suppliers; however, the latter's business failure rate is relatively high.

Finally, American Can and Continental Can have diversified by producing glass and paper board cups; plastic, fibre containers which are substitutable for tin-cans to a degree or possible for future substitutable goods. The two companies are producers of the necessary chemical compounds. For instance, Continental Can owns a tremendous acreage of timberlands. To obtain other raw materials both companies entered the ranks of the one hundred most active acquiring companies among the largest manufacturing companies from 1950 and 1963.[6] For example, Continental acquired the nation's third largest glass container producer, Hazel-Atlas Glass in 1956,[7] and the Robert Gair Company, one of the nation's major producers of shipping containers. According to a recent publication of Continental Can, the company is looking for more than $500 million worth of business. Therefore, similar to the trend of many other big American companies, Amcrican and Continental Cans may not be anxious to strengthen their "classical" monopoly power in only one industry, tin-cans, or to disregard the policies of the Antitrust Administration and of more liberalizing attitudes, deferring the Administration's policy, of the U.S. Supreme Court.

2. Characteristics

Demand for tin-cans (producers' goods) is a derived demand and the cost of tin-cans is only a small fraction of the factor costs of canners. Unlike consumer good industries, there is relatively little product differentiation within the tin-can industry. The priciple means of product

[6]See *Moody's Industrial Manuals* for their acquiring activities and diversification; and also see U.S. Congress, Senate, Sub-committee on Antitrust and Monopoly, *Hearings, Economic Concentration,* Part II, Appendix 5, 6, 9, and 10.

[7]However, the U.S. Supreme Court declared that Continental Can is monopolizing, defining that tin-cans and glass containers are the same line of commerce. See U.S. v. Continental Can Co., *et al.* 84 S. Ct. 1738 (No. 369), 1964.

differentiation lies in the leasing of can-making and can-closing machinery whose patents are dominently held by American and Continental Cans. Particularly, can-closing machinery requires continuous service. Demand for tin-cans is far less vulnerable to business cycles than demand for other producer goods. For example, even during the Great Depression, the value of tin-can shipments did not slacken very much. Per capita demand for tin-cans has grown at a faster rate than per capita growth of the U.S. economy as a whole.[8]

Tin-cans successfully compete with glass, fibre, and plastic containers and, to a degree, with such wrapping materials as plastic bags and films. Glass containers, although readily substitutable for tin-cans for a variety of product uses, offer little direct competition. This is mainly due to the fact that raw glass is more expensive than tin-plates; also, glass containers cost more to ship and stock than tin-cans. Glass containers, however, for certain products may appeal more to consumer tastes, e.g., baby food and instant coffee, regardless of price differences. Paper, fibre, and plastic cans are not suitable for goods which need heat-sterilization or pressure preservation.

> The sensitivity of given metal-can markets to prices of substitutes—the cross elasticity—is generally obscurred by dynamic developments in which one container pushes the other completely or partly out of the field following an innovation in method. The container industry is subject to chronic "packaging revolution."[9]

This statement implies that substitution, if it occurs, is complete in a restricted market. This introduces the factor of zero into cross-elasticity calculation which, of course, makes the measure inapplicable. Therefore, it can be assumed a priori that the demand for tin-cans is a fairly inelastic one. Obviously, this is one of the important criteria in judging empirical results of the various models.

Demand for tin-plate, whose major users are tin-can producers, has grown steadily without any cyclical fluctuation, unlike the demand for many other kinds of steel products. For promotion of their steady business steel companies, in cooperation with tin-can manufacturers, have continuously improved the quality of tin-plate in order to extend its use to many other products. Since World War II, for example, high quality

---

[8]See U.S.Department of Commerce, Bureau of Census, *1963 Census of Manufactures* (Washington, D.C.: Government Printing Office, 1966), MC 63(2)–34A.

[9]James W. McKie, *Tin Cans and Tin Plate* (Cambridge, Mass.: Harvard University Press, 1959), p. 208.

"electrolytic" tin-plate has been produced in increasing quantity, gradually replacing other types of tin-plate. Because of technological improvements, it has become possible to expand the variety of products which can be packed in tin-cans, e.g., beer, motor oil, frozen food, and pressurized products.

On the other hand, a profit squeeze develops in the canning industry when prices for canned products fall, while the can price remains rigid because the buyers market for tin-cans is relatively competitive. Thus canners are placed at a sharp economic disadvantage and have a high failure rate of business.[10] In the end, consumers as well as canners suffer while tin-can producers, mainly American and Continental Can, "fare relatively well." [11]

Price leadership and division of the market prevail in most oligopolistic industries. American Can plays this role in the tin-can industry and has acted as the price leader of the industry since its inception and negotiated prices for tin-plate. (American and Continental Cans were charged with criminal conspiracy and paid fines under the Sherman Act.[12]) American Can has negotiated an annual price for tin-plate and has linked the price of tin-cans to that of tin-plate. Although Continental Can has occasionally rejected American Can's price leadership, after the former became as powerful as its rival in economic power and organization. Generally, however, Continental Can and other can producers have followed American Can's traditional leadership role.

B. QUANTITATIVE STRUCTURE OF THE TIN-CAN INDUSTRY

In this section, we will present four alternative quantitative structural models of the domestic tin-can industry, 1950–1966. The alternative models consist of the ID- and CC-systems as well as the two models of the CCID-system. The main intent is to compare and evaluate the alternative structural models in view of their empirical results. As expressed in the introductory part of this chapter, therefore, all four models will be

---

[10]George W. Stocking, "The Rule of Reason and Monopoly, " George W. Stocking (ed.), *Workable Competition and Anti-trust Policy* (Nashville, Tenn.: Vanderbilt University Press, 1961), p. 176.

[11]*Ibid.*, p. 177.

[12]U.S. v. American Can Company

constructed as similarly as possible instead of vesting a rigorous model for the study of the tin- can industry, per se.

In order to further fair comparison of these competitive systems, this study shall preclude the possibility of different explanatory variables for each system. In other words, a better statistical fit for one system over another shall not be a criterion for the employment of particular explanatory variables. In spite of this prerequisite, it is recognized that some inherent limitations occur as a result of (1) the shortness of economic time series data due to which some explanatory variables cannot be introduced properly; (2) the absense of a clearcut criterion as to which variables have more exogeniety than another.

Therefore, each system of the tin-can industry is analyzed merely on the bases of its three most economically meaningful relations: (1) tin-can supply relations; (2) tin-can demand relations; and (3) market equilibrium relation. Consequently the following model-building is not an endeavor to construct a unique all-embracing theory, but rather to explain the significant forces behind tin-can consumption, output, and price, 1950–1966. (All of the variables are deflated by an appropriate price index which will be explained below.)

The tin-can supply relation correlates total production (annual quantity sold plus change in finished product inventories) to expected gross gain and prices of tin-plate and tin-cans. The expected gross gain is derived from the value added (adj.) minus the payroll of all employees. A lagged gross gain is used as the expected profit based on the assumption that producers (mainly American and Continental) want to maintain a "satisficing" level of gross gain rather than maximization of their profits. Since progressive growth of the tin-can industry has been far less vulnerable to business cycles than the growth of the economy as a whole, the near duopolists, American Can and Continental Can, apparently have been able to maintain their satisficing profit level, at least in the short-run (here short-run is conceived as less than one decade).[13]

In this short-term period, the most important cost involved in tin-can production has been the cost of tin-plate. Labor costs have been approximately only ten percent of the value of production and one fifth of the cost of materials[14](mainly tin-plate). In addition, quality improvements

[13]H. Michael Mann. "Seller Concentration, Barriers to Entry, and Rates of Return in Thirty Industries, 1950–1960, " *Review of Economics and Statistics,* XLVIII (August, 1966), 296–307 and Joe S. Bain, *Barriers to New Competition* (Cambridge: Harvard University Press, 1956), p. 170.

[14]See Bureau of the Census, *1963 Census of Manufactures,* MC 63(2), 34A–6.

in tin-plate have been comparatively marginal since the initiation of the electrolytic method which has gradually replaced the hot dipped method.[15] As a result, the price of tin-plate is employed as a cost index for tin-cans.

Published price data on tin-cans as a whole (particularly before 1950) may be a major shortcoming of any empirical study of the tin-can industry; even the data since 1950 requires a careful selection of an adequate representative category of cans and of the latter's sample period. First, quality improvements and other technological innovations are relatively significant in addition to the fact that the upward real price movement of the average tin-can has been far more than that of tin-plate. Second, a major modification in the specification of cans or a change in the unit of quotations or in the delivery terms introduces a substantial margin of error. Third, a degree of price discrimination has been the prevailing practice of tin-can producers. The price of cans are closely tied with quantity buying, with period contracts (say, for a season) for the purchase of a definite quantity, and with the leasing and servicing of canning machines.

In order to reduce this discrepancy, the price variable for tin-cans is derived as the average price of four representative cans: No. 1, No. 2, No. $2\frac{1}{2}$, and No. 10 tin-cans which are manufactured from $\frac{1}{4}$lb. electrolytic tin-plate with interior enamel by carload lots, f.o.b., Eastern prices which, in turn, are deflated by the *metal container* WPI, BLS Code 10–3, 1957–1959 = 100.

We assume initially that demand for tin-cans is inelastic because it is derived through one or more market layers and because cans are a small cost factor for the canning industry as well as for final consumers. Substitution for tin-cans is possible, but substitutes have not exerted much competitive pressure since the two major producers of tin-cans also produce substitutional containers.

Under competitive conditions, prices should be heavily influenced by any difference between expected demand and supply, as well as by per capita consumer expenditures. However, the tin-can industry approximates a duopoly; so there is sufficient reason to doubt that valid empirical evidence of a short-run price mechanism would be observable. But one can assume that a "normal" price mechanism operates in the long-run,

[15]The electrolytic method was a price reducing factor of tin-plate because the method permitted reduction of tin contents. Tin is a fairly expensive rare metal. The thickness reduction of tin-plate is also a price-reducing factor of tin-plate. Moreover, the price of tin-plate is bilaterally decided by tin-plate producers and tin-can producers; however, the tin-can price is more or less unilaterally decided by the tin-can producers.

even for a monopolist within the framework of a free enterprise system.

Strictly speaking, there is no demand curve for tin-cans, because most of the output goes to large buyers and prices are set by negotiation rather than by market mechanisms. Therefore, tin-can producers are unable to take full advantage of the inelasticity of demand as might be possible if the market were under competition. But both tin-can producers and canners realize that under most circumstances, a cut in tin-can prices, even if fully passed along through lowered canned good prices, does not produce a large enough demand increase to compensate a price cut. Any reduction in the price of tin-cans, even if the final consumer of canned goods were awarded the full benefits would affect only slightly the final price of canned goods and consequently would not have an appreciable effect on the demand for canned goods, e.g., canned food soft drink, beer, etc. The demand for these canned goods, in which most tin-cans find their market, is income inelastic compared to other final consumer goods.

Before constructing alternative models for the tin-can industry, the symbols to be used will be described. In the actual process of adapting the equations, all variables are expressed in logarithmic (base 10) form.

Definitions of Symbols

S_t = the logarithm of the per capita value of tin-can production in year t, deflated by WPI, 1957–59 = 100.

R_{t-1} = the logarithm of one year lagged "profit, " i.e., the value added (adjusted) by the industry minus payroll of all employees, deflated by WPI, 1957–59 = 100. Lagged profit is assumed at a "satisficing" level of expected gain of the industry.

P_t = the logarithm of the average price of No. 1, No. 2, No. $2\frac{1}{2}$ and No. 10 tin-cans ($\frac{1}{4}$ 1b. electrolytic tin-plate, interior enamel) per thousand can bulk, in carload lots, f.o.b. Eastern prices in year t, deflated by metal container WPI (BLS Code 10–13), 1957–59 = 100.

TP_t = the logarithm of the price of $\frac{1}{4}$ 1b. electrolytic tin-plate 14 × 20 per 1000 1bs. in year t, deflated by finished steel products WPI (BLS Code 1014), 1957–59 = 100. (Code 1014 was changed to 101302 in January, 1967.)

D_t = the logarithm of the per capital vaue of the tin-can consumption in year t, deflated by WPI, 1957–59 = 100.

T = trend variables.

Y_t = the logarithm of per capita personal consumption expenditures in 1958 dollars in year t.

u_{it} = is a disturbance term with i = 1,2,3.

Parameters to be evaluated from the data are: a_i, b_i, and c_i with i = 0,1,2,3 for a_i and b_i, and with i = 0,1,2 for c_i. Accordingly, a_o and b_o are the intercept of the supply and demand relations, respectively for all the systems; and c_o is an intercept of the price mechanism relation in the CC-system. Coefficients a_i with i = 1,2,3 is the supply "elasticity" of T, TP and P, respectively. Coefficients b_i with i = 1,2 is the demand "elasticity" with respect to income and with respect to price and should be positive and negative, respectively. b_3 is a coefficient for a simple trend variable T in the ID- and CC-systems; b_3, in the Bicausal-Chain system is the coefficient of a lagged D_t. In the price mechanism (3) of the CC-system, c_1 is the coefficient of Y and c_2 is the coefficient for the gap between assumed *ex ante* supply and *ex ante* demand; and c_2 should be less than one so as to have a convergence.

S_t, D_t, and P_t are assumed as jointly dependent variables; and the rest of the variables are assumed as predetermined variables. The assumption for P_t is necessitated by a technical complexity in the construction of analogous competing systems. This appeared to be a contradiction to the findings above. It was found that the price of tin-cans was set at an administered level by the powerful producers instead of short-term market forces. However, it has been intuitively argued that the market forces should dominate the price at least in the long-run under our free enterprise system. And also the administered price itself should be heavily influenced by the market forces in the course of administrative decision-making processes.

1. The ID-System

A simple ID-model for the tin-can market is constructed as,

(1) $S = a_o + a_1 R_{-1} + a_2 TP + a_3 P + u_1$ (Supply relation)

Table 1

The Annual Time Series for the Variables and Price Deflators

YEAR	VARIABLE					
	S ($)	R ($1000)	P ($)	TP ($)	D ($)	Y ($)
1950	—	196,138	60.8989	—	8.1442	
1951	8.3050	202,731	54.9560	10.4399	7.9196	1509
1952	8.5422	228,989	53.9025	10.4161	8.1794	1525
1953	9.3050	263,853	53.9988	9.8667	8.9461	1572
1954	9.5769	274,784	53.8342	9.4885	9.1208	1575
1955	9.8790	337,815	54.2475	9.2796	9.4524	1659
1956	10.5828	367,360	53.7346	9.2117	10.1342	1673
1957	10.4436	361,277	54.5541	8.8786	9.9520	1683
1958	10.9001	363,268	54.9135	8.7575	10.3889	1666
1959	11.2783	334,158	55.8801	8.8954	10.8093	1735
1960	11.1300	330,215	55.4737	8.9128	10.6424	1749
1961	11.8716	409,882	55.7598	8.9449	11.3684	1755
1962	11.7371	400,652	56.0969	8.9744	11.2498	1813
1963	11.5144	452,128	55.8763	8.8954	10.9220	1865
1964	12.3207	529,180	56.1456	8.8521	11.6825	1946*
1965	12.6117**	574,685	56.3129	8.8461	12.0083**	2036*
1966	13.2815**	563,282	56.4136	8.7202	12.6229**	2111*
1967	N.A.	663,525#	56.9544#	8.8763#	.9506#	2162

N.A. stands for "not available"

Statistics for Industry Groups and Industries: Series MC 67(*P*)-1, Apri*rt*, 9.*o*961l,

#The data are based on *1967 Census of Manufactures, PrelimRepinary*

Table 1—*Continued*

YEAR	PRICE DEFLATOR WPI-103	WPI-1014	WPI	POPULATION (1000)
1950	71.2	63.1	86.8	152,271
1951	78.9	68.2	96.7	154,878
1952	79.5	69.7	94.0	157,553
1953	82.9	75.0	92.7	160,184
1954	85.1	78.2	92.9	163,026
1955	86.6	81.9	93.2	165,931
1956	92.2	88.8	96.2	168,903
1957	98.5	97.2	99.0	171,984
1958	101.4	100.6	100.4	174,882
1959	100.2	102.3	100.6	177,830
1960	100.3	102.1	100.7	180,684
1961	102.0	101.7	100.3	183,756
1962	103.7	101.4	100.6	186,656
1963	104.7	102.3	100.3	189,417
1964	105.5	102.8	100.5	192,120
1965	107.6	103.3	102.5	194,583*
1966	110.0	104.7	105.9	196,842*
1967	111.8	105.9	106.1	199,188

Sources of data: U.S. Dept. of Commerce, Bureau of the Census, *1963 Census of Manufactures* (Wash. D.C.: Government Printing Office, 1966), MC 63(2)–34A and *Annual Survey of Manufactures* (up to 1966 issues); U.S. Dept. of Commerce, *Business Statistics* (1967 Biennial Ed.); *Economic Report of the President*, Appendix B, 1967; U.S. Dept. of Labor, Bureau of Labor Statistics, *Wholesale Prices and Price Index* (up to 1967 series); and *Metal Statistics* (New York: American Metal Market, up to 1968 ed.).

*Figures are slightly revised in 1968.

**Figures need slight revision due to revised figures of population.

(2) $D = b_o + b_1Y + b_2P + b_3T + u_2$ (Demand relation)

(3) $S = D = Q$ (Equilibrium assumption)

(Time subscript t is not shown for convenience.)

As was described in detail in Chapter III, the coefficient matrix of the endogenous variables is:

$$\begin{bmatrix} 1 & -a_3 \\ 1 & -b_2 \end{bmatrix}$$

thereby showing the model to be interdependent.

Equations (1) and (2) cannot be estimated directly by the least-squares method because the equations cannot be specified in terms of conditional expectations, i.e.,

(1-a) $E(S/R_{-1},TP,P) \neq a_o + a_1R_{-1} + a_2TP + a_3P$

(2-a) $E(D/Y,P) \neq b_o + b_1Y + b_2P + b_3T$

The two stage least-squares method is used in estimating the coefficients of the supply and demand relations.

Equations (1) and (2) are both overidentified since the two predetermined variables, Y and T, do not appear in (1), and R_{-1} and TP do not appear in (2). In other words, the number of predetermined variables excluded from the relation is greater than the included number of endogenous variables less one. After the model is cast in the reduced form, the rank order condition is tested. (1) and (2) are overidentified respectively. The rank of the reduced form coefficient matrix is greater than the included number of endogenous variables less one.

The last relation (3), the assumption of $S = D = Q$, should not be mistaken as an identity condition. As has been argued in earlier chapters, even if the identity postulate and equilibrium assumption appear to be the same in their notational formality, they are distinct entities, S and D are defined in terms of their variables in relation (2) and (3), respectively; consequently, the third relation (3) distinguishes clearly the term S and D as individual functions, rather than specifying the ex-post value of S to be identical with that of D. In short, (3) is implemented as an equilibrium assumption imposed between (1) and (2) so as to build a typical ID-system.

It can be argued, on the other hand, that (3) can be postulated as an identity and expressed in a truistic statement, such as (3a) $S = D - I$, instead of (3) where "I" denotes inventory change. For the above model, however, the implementation of (3a) will create peculiar complications for the ID-system, unless an adequate functional relation for "I" is specified in the model.[16] Although this direction of investigation may be worthwhile, it is not pursued here because of its statistically insignifi-

[16]If (3a) is eliminated by substitution, the following results can be seen:

(1–A) $Q^s = a_o + a_1R_{-1} + a_2TP + a_3P - u_1$

(2–A) $Q^s = b_o + b_1Y + b_2P + b_3T + (u_2 - I)$

(1–B) $Q^d = a_o + a_1R_{-1} + a_2TP + a_3P + (u_1 + I)$

(2–B) $Q^d = b_o + b_1Y + b_2P + b_3T + u_2$

Furthermore, from the above systems (A) and (B), three combinative systems can be implied also.

cant results from a test run. Perhaps, it is necessary to collect new data to employ other variables for the implementation of (3a) in the model. Therefore, (3) seems to fulfill our comparative purposes by simply comparing typical models of both the ID- and CC-systems rather than specific ones.

In the system, (1) (2) (3), either the quantity demanded, D, or supplied, S, can be chosen to represent Q in the system, because D and S are not equal in value in general. As a result, there are two relations explaining one and the same thing.[17] In specific, the two alternative reduced forms

$$S = f(R_{-1},TP,Y,T) + w_1 \text{ and } D = F(R_{-1},TP,Y,T) + w_2$$

(where w_1 or w_2 stands for the composite disturbance term, u_{-1} and u_2) show only a slight difference due to the small difference between the actual values of S and D for the industry (see below including footnote 18). Here S is arbitrarily chosen to represent Q in order to maintain consistency in its future use.

Since the reduced form can be specified in terms of conditional expectations, the least-squares method is applied to them. The results are:

$$(4)\quad P = \underset{(.2870)}{1.3991} - \underset{(.0511)}{0.0445}R_{-1} + \underset{(.2241)}{0.1279}TP + \underset{(.1376)}{0.2622}Y - \underset{(.0173)}{0.0053}T$$

$R^2 = .7111$
$F = 6.77$
$SEE = .0048$
$DW = .84$

The figures in parentheses are the standard errors of the regression coefficients; R^2 is the square of the multiple correlation coefficient; SEE is the standard error of estimates; F is the F-distribution; and DW is the Durbin-Watson statistic of serial correlation. (Hereafter the same notations will be used for each regression equation.)

$$(5)^{18}\quad Q^s = \underset{(.7079)}{-0.6656} + \underset{(.1115)}{0.0150}R_{-1} - \underset{(.4891)}{0.3252}TP + \underset{(.3303)}{0.5565}Y + \underset{(.0378)}{0.0775}T$$

[17]It is quite surprising that no econometrician has mentioned the problem. After receiving a critique on this subject from my major Professor Franklin V. Walker, State University of New York, I noticed that George Stojkovic in his paper, "Market Models for Agricultural Products, " Ch. 13 in Herman Wold ed. *Econometric Model Building* (Amsterdam: North-Holland Publishing Co., 1964), pp. 402–3, has briefly mentioned the problem in passing.

[18]Alternatively, if Q represents D instead of S,

$$(5a)\quad Q^d = \underset{(.7595)}{-0.5882} + \underset{(.1196)}{0.0135}R_{-1} - \underset{(.5248)}{0.2655}TP + \underset{(.3222)}{0.5111}Y + \underset{(.0406)}{0.0854}T$$

$R^2 = .9766$
$SEE = .0105$
$F = 114.78$
$DW = 2.44$

The reduced equation forms, (4), (5), and (5a), will be directly interpreted from a statistical point of view in terms of conditional expectations. No economic meaning, however, can be given to coefficients of reduced forms. They are included only for purposes of estimation, and their value is judged only by the forecasts for the observed value (Q).

The structural equation for the *supply relation* is subsequently estimated as,

$$(6) \quad S = \underset{(1.6071)}{-5.4388} + \underset{(.0869)}{0.1231R_{-1}} - \underset{(.3010)}{0.8397TP} + \underset{(1.2180)}{3.5775\ddot{P}}$$

$R^2 = .9626$
$SEE = .0127$
$F = 102.98$
$DW = 2.09$

where the umlaut ¨ over P indicates the calculated value of P from (4). The calculated value of P is substituted for P in (1). Except for R_{-1}, the correlation and regression coefficients are significant and the standard errors shown are asymptotic.[19] All coefficients have appropriate signs. Interpretation of the statistical equation (6) indicates that the production of tin-cans varies directly with the expected profits (R_{-1}) of the tightly-knit oliogopolists, as well as with the price of tin-cans ($\ddot{P}$), and inversely with the cost index of the major raw material (TP).

In contrast to this numerical magnitude, however, the price elasticity of supply appears to be smaller in light of our previously stated a priori theory. It was assumed that the supply of tin-cans would be inelastic with respect to the price of tin-cans, and that profit expectations were

---

$R^2 = .9725$
$SEE = .0113$
$F = 97.14$
$DW = 2.35$

The two alternative reduced forms show only a slight difference due to the minimal difference between the actual values of S and D for industry. (5) and (5a) will be employed separately for the purpose of prediction in the next chapter.

[19] It should be noted that the regression equation is not a simple interpolation. Correlation and standard errors are presented only as measures of goodness of fit.

fixed by the two giants. Second, it was assumed that the giant tin-can Producers would deemphasize the production of tin-cans in the event that expected profits were not at a satisficing level. Moreover, it was assumed that the tightly-knit oligopolists' production of tin-cans would be influenced very little by their own administered prices. In the light of these assumptions, therefore, we believe the elasticity of supply (P) is much too high.

This result of an inelastic coefficient of TP, however, is not surprising, because TP is set by negotiations between tin-can and tin-plate industries in a joint decision-making process. For sixteen observations of time series data and three independent variables, the boundary of the Durbin-Watson statistic becomes 0.86 – 1.73 at the 5% significance level.[20] Hence, one can accept the hypothesis that the true residuals are serially uncorrelated and that the F-ratio is asymptotically significant.

The original structural equation for the *demand relation* is subsequently estimated as,

$$(7) \qquad D = \underset{(3.2711)}{-0.2263} + \underset{(.4426)}{0.5460Y} - \underset{(2.6399)}{0.3582\ddot{P}} + \underset{(.0180)}{0.1109T}$$

$$\begin{aligned} R^2 &= .9709 \\ SEE &= .0111 \\ F &= 133.49 \\ DW &= 2.32 \end{aligned}$$

where the calculated value of P ($\ddot{P}$) from (4) is substituted for P in (2).

As the above result indicates, the price as well as the income elasticity have proper signs and that their numerical magnitudes are plausible. These facts confirm the a priori theory and verify the correlation as significant. However, the standard error for the price elasticity is too large to permit a definite stand on the "elasticity pessimism" controversy. The Durbin-Watson coefficient indicates an inconclusive region in the negative serial correlation (i.e., 0.05 short of accepting the hypothesis that the true residuals are serially uncorrelated); although, the coefficient is very near the upper boundary.

Even though the price elasticity of demand, obtained by employing the "notoriously inadequate price indexes," is not significant, results are probably as good as can be expected. This limitation is primarily due to

[20]J. Durbin and G. S. Watson, "Testing for Serial Correlation in Least-Squares Regression, " Part II, *Biometrika*, XXXVIII (June, 1951), 173, table 4.

the paucity of observations and the relatively few fluctuations in the real price of tin-cans during the period. Second, the results are the best obtainable in view of the fact that the effect of tin-can prices on demand is relatively long-term. The predictability of short-term price elasticity is low. This may be intuitively correct, because if short-term adjustments for the final consumers are assumed difficult to make quickly in response to price increases in the canning industry, it follows that demand should be inelastic in the short-run. Perhaps then prices do not contribute enough for an adequate explanation of tin-can demand; conseqently, the influence of prices is found to be statistically insignificant. This fact is partially verified by the results.

Needless to explain in detail, the time trend (T) was simply introduced in the demand relation as representing all slowly changing forces not accounted for by the other variables. The coefficient of T is statistically significant and thus is an important result. It implies the rejection of the null hypothesis and gives "trend" a prominent role in the demand relation.[21]

2. The CC-System

A simple CC-system for the tin-can industry model is constructed in substantive aspects as similarly as possible to the ID-system—

(1) $$S = a_o + a_1 R_{-1} + a_2 TP + a_3 P_{-1} + u_1 \quad \text{(Supply)}$$

---

[21]If T is excluded from relation (2) and subsequently from (7), the results are far less satisfactory than those of (7) since

(7a) $D = -0.8674 + 1.5399Y - 1.7858\ddot{P}$
(6.8985) (.8268) (5.4719)

$R^2 = .8748$
$SEE = .0222$
$F = 45.40$
$DW = 0.68$

Both coefficients appear to be much higher than expected in the a priori theory, regardless of their proper signs. The higher elasticities are due to the very strong trend in the demand for tin-cans. When the trend in the explanatory variables is stronger than the trend in the explained variable, elasticity will be overstated.

The low DW coefficient may be due to serial correlation of the disturbance terms and/or omitted variables. In other words, if both these omitted variables and the dependent variable are serially correlated, it is likely that the omitted variables also will be correlated with the lagged value of the dependent variable.

Consequently, (7) is proved to be a far better specification of the model than (7a).

(2) $$D = b_o + b_1Y + b_2P + b_3T + u_2 \quad \text{(Demand)}$$

(3) $$P = c_o + c_1Y + c_2(D_{-1} - S) + u_3 \quad \text{(Price)}$$

(The time subscript t is not shown for convenience.)

Relations (1) and (2) are exactly the same as in the ID-system except that the lagged price variable in (1) is employed instead of the current price variable.

The above relations are based on several assumptions. Assuming disequilibrium between supply and demand, a major difference between the ID- and CC-systems is that the price relation (or price mechanism) in

Figure 11.
The arrow scheme specification of the CC-model for the tin-can industry

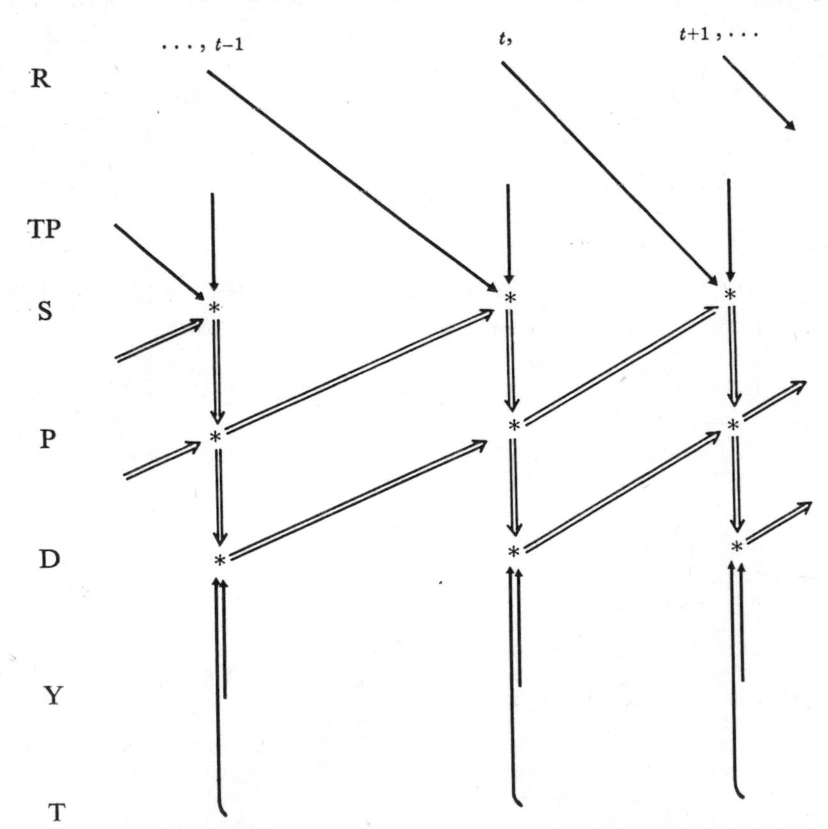

(3) is constructed as an explicit relation in the CC-system.[22] The price variable is assumed to be significantly influenced by Y and *ex ante* excess demand. Furthermore, *ex ante* supply is assumed as approximately the same as the current year's supply and *ex ante* demand is assumed to be approximately the same as the previous year's demand.

As was explained, an arrow scheme specification of the model, (1)-(3), is necessary for the CC-system. In Figure 11 below the double-line arrows indicate a flow of causation among the current and lagged endogenous variables; the single line arrows indicate the causal influences of the exogenous variables. Specifically, S is causally explained by P_{-1}, R_{-1}, and Y; P is explained by the expected excess demand and Y; and D is explained by Y, P, and T. The reason for the inclusion of T is the same as for the ID-system. Distinct from the ID-system, however, the arrows flow in only unidirection in the order of equation (1), (3) and (2). Its subdiagonal matrix of the current endogenous variables is:

$$\begin{bmatrix} 0 & 0 & 0 \\ -c_2 & 0 & 0 \\ 0 & b_2 & 0 \end{bmatrix}$$

Therefore, each relation can be specified as conditional expectations:

(1a) $$E(S/R_{-1}, TP, P_{-1}) = a_o + a_1 R_{-1} + a_2 TP + a_3 P_{-1}$$

(3a) $$E[P/Y, (D_{-1} - S)] = c_o + c_1 Y + c_2(D_{-1} - S)$$

(2a) $$E(D/Y, P, T) = b_o + b_1 Y + b_2 P + b_3 T$$

Consequently, the above three relations, (1)–(3), in the CC-system can be directly estimated by the method of least-squares.

(4) $$\underset{}{S} = \underset{(0.9193)}{-1.3287} + \underset{(.0757)}{0.3009R_{-1}} - \underset{(.4196)}{0.7097TP} + \underset{(.3725)}{0.2740P_{-1}}$$

$R^2 = .9386$
$SEE = .0163$
$F = 61.12$
$DW = 1.41$

All coefficients have proper signs as in the ID-system. The coefficient of the expected profit level is significant and its standard error is asy-

[22]For detailed arguments for the price mechanism, see Chapters II and IV.

mptotic unlike in the ID-system. The expected profit of the industry satisfactorily explains the amount of production, confirming the previously stated a priori theory. Thus, the supply behavior of the tightly-knit near duopolists can be well explained by a satisficing level of their gains. However, the standard error of the coefficient of TP is slightly lower than an asymptotic level; the standard error of coefficient of P_{-1} is particularly unsatisfactory, unlike in the ID-system. The DW coefficient is inconclusive.

It becomes obvious that the supply relation of the ID-system is a better measure of goodness of fit than that of the CC-system, except the coefficient of R_{-1}. However, the relatively poor performance of the latter is mainly due to a technicality in building similar compeiting systems for comparative purposes. Therefore, if the study were not comparative but an econometric model of the tin-can industry, the current P would be employed instead of the lagged P, in accordance with a priori information. That is, in reality, prices are administered variously because they emerge from the producers' decision-making processes, at least in the short-run, rather than being decided by market forces.

Therefore, in order to demonstrate a flexibility of the CC-system beyond a strict comparison to the above ID-system, the following results are presented with P specified as an explanatory variable for the supply relation in the short-run. Its theoretical basis for estimation is the corollary to this author's theorem 1 in Chapter IV. This direction of investigation will be heavily emphasized to distinguish short-run phenomena from long-run ones in my forthcoming research paper.[23] Without presenting any results of this investigation, however, the main purpose of this comparative study can be sufficiently maintained.

$$(4a) \quad S = -3.1599 + \underset{(.0714)}{0.2328R_{-1}} - \underset{(.3161)}{0.6858TP} + \underset{(.7313)}{1.6461P}$$

$$R^2 = .9549$$
$$SEE = .0140$$
$$F = 84.62$$
$$DW = 1.84$$

In this situation, the magnitude of the coefficient of R_{-1} is very reasonable and its standard error is asymptotic unlike in the ID-system. Although the magnitude of the price elasticity is a bit larger than the a priori theory, it is less than half of its counterpart in the ID-system. The Durbin-Waston

[23]The project is supported by the State University of New York Research Foundation.

coefficient indicates no serial correlation. In spite of the fact that the employment of P_{-1} in the relation gives a disadvantage to the CC-system, relation (4) rather than (4a) is maintained here as the supply relation in order to provide room for fair judgement by individual readers and to prevent criticism from ID-oriented econometricians. Note that the CC-system was demonstrated as theoretically sounder than other competing systems in the previous chapters.

As Y increases there is more room for a margin between prices and production costs, and prices tend to go up due to creeping expense inflation regardless of technological innovations.[24]

$$\text{(5)} \qquad \underset{}{P} = \underset{(.0812)}{1.2453} + \underset{(.0674)}{0.1170}(D_{-1} - S) + \underset{(.0252)}{0.1543}Y$$

$$R^2 = .7486$$
$$SEE = .0041$$
$$F = 19.36$$
$$DW = 1.23$$

The coefficient of the excess demand in equation (5) is not significant; however, the two coefficients indicate the appropriate signs. The coefficient of Y is significant at the 99% level. The price is influenced by the excess demand. Price movement depends upon the size of the gap between the industry's expected production and the consumers' expected demand and per capita consumption expenditure. Even though the industry is tightly controlled by the powerful producers, the industry operates in the long-run within the framework of a market economy. That is, no matter what kind of monopoly power is held by the giant companies, the market mechanism tends in the long-run to govern the economic variables of the tin-can industry in a free enterprise system. Also, growth of the economy as well as of tin-can demand may tend to reduce the barriers to new industry entries. As a result, many growing canners have begun to produce their own cans. For instance, the Campbell Soup Company, which purchased its cans from Continental Can, is the nation's third largest tin-can producer today. (Campbell Soup's production is all captive cans.)

Needless to say many other variables beside Y and $(D_{-1} - S)$ influence a price determination strategy of American and Continental Cans. How-

[24] Employees of major can producers belong to many highly organized trade unions. They belong to Steel Workers, Mechanist, International Electrical Workers, Printing and Lithographic Workers, Plumbers, etc., which are under the "union shop" charter, respectively, according to their fields of work in a plant.

ever these variables are not included in the projected model because of their multicollinearity, available data, degree of freedom, etc.

Following the arrow scheme specification of the model one can derive a vector regression form (the reduced form of the CC-system) by replacing S by the calculated value of S from (4). This replacement is valid because the price relation in (5) involves the explanatory endogenous variable S.

$$\text{(5a)} \quad P = \underset{(.0695)}{1.2826} + \underset{(.0593)}{0.1785}(D_{-1} - \ddot{S}) + \underset{(.0214)}{0.1434}Y$$

$$R^2 = .8174$$
$$SEE = .0035$$
$$F = 29.10$$
$$DW = 1.36$$

where the umlaut ¨ in S indicates the calculated value of S from the relation (4). Note that the legitimacy of both (5) and (5a) can be found in the Wold Proximity Theorem. In specific, (5) is based on the corollary to the author's theorem 1 and (5a), on the theorem; both (5) and (5a) are actually generalizations of the proximity theorem.

The results are more promising than (5). Both coefficients are asymptotically significant at the 1% level. F-distribution and DW are slightly better, while DW is still inconclusive. The improved results may be caused by the indirect influence of such important variables as TP and R_{-1} in (4) on the price mechanism. Unlike (4) in the ID-system, the economic meaning is clear in the reduced form of the CC-system and in its forecasts of the variables.

Regarding the demand relation (2) when the least-square method is applied, one derives

$$\text{(6)} \quad D = \underset{(.8506)}{-1.6163} + \underset{(.1604)}{0.3669}Y + \underset{(.6098)}{0.7725}P + \underset{(.0160)}{0.1129}T$$

$$R^2 = .9761$$
$$SEE = .0101$$
$$F = 163.43$$
$$DW = 2.54$$

The effect of demand on positive price elasticity is negligent. Treatment of this problem, similar to Henry L. Moore's paradox,[25] must be based

[25] See his *Economic Cycles, Their Laws and Cause* (New York: The Macmillan, 1914), p. 114; also see Elmer Working, "What Do Statistical 'Demand Curves' Show?," *Quarterly Journal of Economics*, XLIII (February, 1927), 227.

on knowledge of the industry and economic reasoning, not merely upon the "notoriously inadequate price index" itself. The price index can only produce results which more or less approximate intersections of the shifting supply and demand relations that represent neither a demand relation nor a supply relation. This failure does not mean that such curves for intersections are not useful. For instance, if changes in demand relations cause changes in supply, or vice versa, it may be more useful to know what the price-quantity relationship is under those conditions, than to know what the elasticity of demand or supply is.

This reasoning is valid because, as was mentioned, the demand for tin-cans has grown more steadily than the average growth of the economy. Therefore, the price can be expected to exert less of an influence on demand at higher income levels, because income becomes less of a constraining factor and canned goods are partly subject to "habit formation."[26] On the other hand, equation (6) indicates that the demand has shifted far more than supply. Thus since price is of the administered variety, output rather than price would be expected to vary. Of course, if output radically were to fall below expectations such that the expected profit level were also disappointing, the oligopolists might lower their price; but even this adjustment probably would be partial and slow.

Moreover, if prices were very rigid, no estimate of price elasticity of demand could be obtained,[27] even if the price index were not "notoriously inadequate." Such a condition would be ideal for the estimation of income elasticity of demand and it could be expected to provide better estimates of the demand relation.[28]

When the explanatory endogenous variable P is replaced by its calculated value from (5), in conformity with this author's theorem 1 in Chapter IV, the reduced form of the CC-system is derived as,

---

[26]This is explained below in "Some Remarks . . ." on pp. 130 ff.

[27]See for example, O.W. Main, *The Canadian Nickel Industry* (Toronto: University of Toronto Press, 1955), pp. 114f.

[28]In this tin-can industry,

$$D = -0.6660 + 0.4891Y + 0.1114T$$
$$\quad (.4266) \quad (.1355) \quad (.0169)$$

$R^2 = .9709$
$SEE = .107$
$F = 216.58$
$DW = 2.34$

The standard errors shown are asymptotic and the DW coefficient indicates no serial correlation. The coefficient of Y is very close to that of Y in (6). Then, it may be ideal for the estimation of income elasticity of demand only for the tin-can industry. That is, it might be a better idea to extrude the price variable from the empirical testing.

$$(7) \quad D = 0.7984 + 0.6526Y - 1.2455\ddot{P} + 0.1122T$$
$$\qquad (3.0331) \quad (.3631) \quad (2.3476) \quad (.0175)$$

$$R^2 = .9714$$
$$SEE = .0110$$
$$F = 136.0$$
$$DW = 2.17$$

where the umlaut ¨ above P indicates the calculated value of P from relation (5). The theoretical legitimacy of (6) as well as of (7) are found in the above mentioned generalization of the Wold Proximity Theorem.

The results are far more promising than (6) and both income and price elasticity have proper signs; however, the standard error of the price elasticity is too large to be reliable.

3. The CCID-System

As has been discussed in detail, the CCID-system can be classified as (A) the Bicausal Chain system and (B) the Circular Chain system. These subsystems are considered separately below and independently compared to the ID- and CC- systems.

a. The Bicausal Chain System

A simple bicausal chain system for the tin-can industry is constructed as similarly as possible to both the ID- and CC-systems above, solely for the purpose of comparative study,

$$(1) \quad S = a_o + a_1R_{-1} + a_2TP + a_3P_{-1} + u_1 \quad \text{(Supply)}$$

$$(2) \quad D = b_o + b_1Y + b_2P + b_3T + u_2 \quad \text{(Demand)}$$

$$(3) \quad S = D = Q \quad \text{(Equilibrium)}$$

(The time subscript t is not shown for writing simplicity.)

The supply relation (1) is identical to that in the CC-system, (or alternatively the same as that in the ID-system if this author's corollary to theorem 1 in Chapter IV is applied). Second, the demand relation (2) and equilibrium assumption (3) in its appearance, is exactly the same as in the ID-system. However, the system is causally specified according to the arrow scheme as follows:

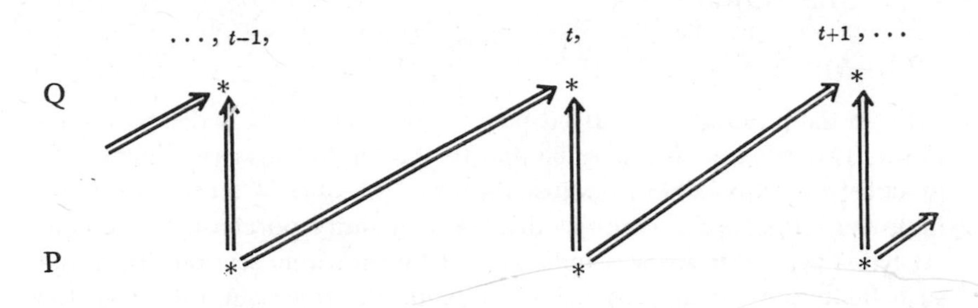

(For simplicity, the influence of exogenous variables are not shown in the above diagram.)

Thus, the arrows indicate a flow of causation among the current and the lagged endogenous variables. The coefficient matrix of the endogenous variables becomes:

$$\begin{bmatrix} 1 & 0 \\ 1 & b_2 \end{bmatrix}$$

The system, therefore, adopts the formal property of the ID-system, but is specified in line with the following arrow pattern:

(4) $$E(Q^s/R_{-1},TP,P_{-1}) = a_o + a_1R_{-1} + a_2TP + a_3P_{-1}$$

(5) $$E(Q^d/Y,P,T) = b_o + b_1Y + b_2P + b_3T$$

Specification (5) is based on this author's corollary to theorem 1 in Chapter IV. Specification (4) is the same as in the CC-system; hence, its result is the same as (4) in the CC-system above. Assuming these specifications are adequate, the ordinary least-squares regression can be applied to (4) and (5), respectively.

(6) $$\underset{}{Q^s} = \underset{(.9193)}{-1.3287} + \underset{(.0757)}{0.3009R_{-1}} - \underset{(.4196)}{0.7097TP} + \underset{(.3725)}{0.2740P_{-1}}$$

$R^2 = .9386$
$SEE = .0163$
$F = 61.12$
$DW = 1.84$

$$(7) \quad Q^d = -1.6163 + 0.3669Y + 0.7725P + 0.1129T$$
$$\qquad\qquad (.8506) \quad (.1604) \quad (.6098) \quad (.0160)$$

$$R^2 = .9761$$
$$SEE = .0101$$
$$F = 163.43$$
$$DW = 2.54$$

From these results the derived positive price elasticity is disappointing in (7). This consequence may be due to the "notorious price index." In practice it is impossible to adjust the price variable in terms of quality improvements, special contract discount, quantity purchasing discount, etc.; this price rigidity was indicated in the previous section. To avoid such limitations, it may be better to exude the price variable from the system as has been done in many well-known studies,[29] which assume that the above facts are true and serious. On the other hand, according to an investigation by Houthakker and Taylor of U.S. consumption, if the commodity consumption is subject to strong "habit formation," the positive price elasticity may be appropriate.[30]

In addition, the negative price elasticity and improvements in the t-values for price and income coefficients are quite attractive. Additional information on a "habit formation" in the use of canned goods is indicated by the positive coefficient of the lagged demand variable, D_{-1}. Houthakker and Taylor state in their *Consumer Demand* that

> . . . habit formation quite clearly predominates in the United States consumption. . . . Quite clearly, if income levels are high enough, it is possible for all commodities to become subject to habit formation. Our results indicate that the United States may be well along toward this end . .
>
> Prices, on the other hand, are much less important . . . in explaining United States consumption. . . .
>
> The lack of a strong overall influence of prices is consistent with the predominance of habit formation. Prices should be expected to exert less of an influence on consumption at high levels of income because income

---

[29]For example, see H.S. Houthakker and Lester D. Taylor, *Consumer Demand in the United States, 1929–1970: Analysis and Projections* (Cambridge: Harvard University Press, 1966), pp. 15 impasse; also see Franklin M. Fisher, *A Priori Information and Time Series Analysis: Essays in Economic Theory and Measurement* (Amsterdam: North-Holland Publishing Co., 1962), p. 97.

[30]*Ibid.*, pp. 97 and 101.

Many canned commodities might be subject to "habit formation" in many ways; however, the degree of habit formation may justify positive price elasticity for canned commodities. It would be a worthwhile investigation for future research to ascertain the degree of "habit formation" that could justify positive price elasticity.

becomes less of a constraining factor and because more commodities become subject to habit formation.[31]

In this case, however, the positive price elasticity introduces inadequacies, and it might be correct to conclude the bicausal chain system as inferior to the ID- and CC-systems for purposes of describing the tin-can industry. Of course, the judgement could be different if the constraint of constructing similar models were removed from the study. Thus, it might be too hasty to reject the bicausal chain system which, as was earlier stated, certainly possesses definite merits in its own right. Consequently, it would be worthwhile to rebuild the bicausal chain system by discarding the constraint of building a similar model to the ID- and CC-system.

To attain this goal, the lagged demand variable, D_{t-1}, will be employed as an explanatory variable to replace the trend variable in the demand relation (2). The results are:

$$(8)\quad D_t = \underset{(1.6169)}{0.3101} + \underset{(.2434)}{0.5157Y} - \underset{(1.0123)}{0.9723P} + \underset{(.1891)}{0.7244D_{t-1}} + w_t$$

$R^2 = .9439$
$SEE = .0154$
$F = 61.31$
$DW = 2.48 +$ biases[32]

These results are not only far more promising than (7) which involved positive price elasticity, but are also slightly more promising than those of both the ID- and CC-system. For these reasons, the bicausal chain model will be rebuilt as if this were not a comparative study. The only deficiencies in the new model will be the "distributed lag" bias or "serial correlation" bias in the parameters including the Durbin-Watson coefficient. These deficiences will be discussed later.

According to the arrow scheme specification of the model, the employment of D_{-1} in place of T is easily constructed as

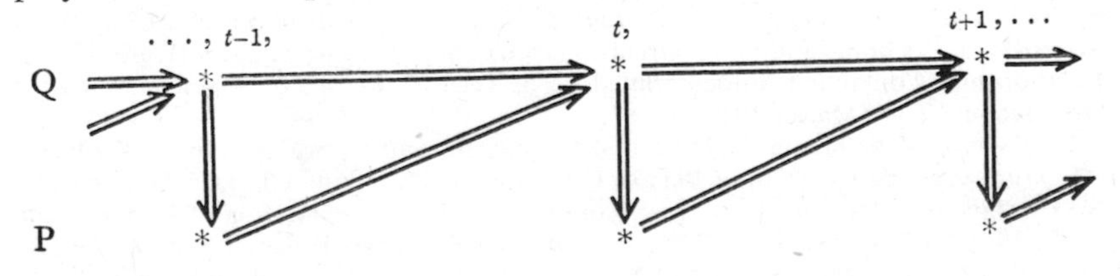

[31]Houthakker and Taylor, *Consumer Demand*, p. 152.
[32]See "Some Remarks . . . " below.

As was stated before, the influence of the exogenous variables are not shown above for simplicity.

The new specification of the model is justifiable if the naive first order autoregressive equation is assumed to be in line with the Cochrane-Orcutt study.[33] The model is also justified by the smooth upward trend of D_t with relatively minor fluctuations,

$$\text{i.e., } D_t = bD_{t-1} + e_t$$

where $e_t = re_{t-1} + \varepsilon_t$. Of course variables are assumed to be measured as deviations from their mean values, and ε_t is assumed to be an independently distributed random variable with a finite and small constant variance for all t.

When sixteen time series data for D_t is applied,

$$8(a) \quad D = \underset{(.0750)}{0.0476} + \underset{(.0750)}{0.9643}D_{t-1} + \ddot{e}_t$$

$$R^2 = .9219$$
$$SEE = .0169$$
$$F = 165.35$$
$$DW = 2.38 + 2[r(1 - b^2)/(1 + br)].$$[34]

Although there are biases in the parameters and other calculated statistics in these results, D_t "can be explained by trend alone without resort to economic theory."[35]

1. Some remarks on bicausal-chain resultant biases: "distributed lag" and "serial correlation"

The results of (8) should not be overlooked because of the very serious biases produced by the lagged variable, D_{t-1}, in conjunction with an autocorrelated disturbance. In addition, it is highly probable that D_{t-1} and

---

[33]An original investigation was done by G. H. Orcutt in his "A Study of the Autoregressive Nature of the Time Series Used for Tinbergen's Model of the Economic System of the United States, 1919–1932," *Journal of the Royal Statistical Society*, CXI (1948), Series B; D. Cochrane and G. H. Orcutt, "Application of Least Squares Regressions to Relationships Containing Autocorrelated Error Terms," *Journal of American Statistical Association*, XLIV (March, 1949), 32–61.

[34]This asymptotic bias in the Durbin-Watson coefficient is developed by Ziv Griliches, "A Note on Serial Correlation Bias in Estimates of Distributed Lags," *Econometrica*, XXIX (January, 1961), 65f. Griliches' work is done by the suggestion of J. Durbin and G. S. Watson's famous article, "Testing for Serial Correlation in Least-Squares Regression," Pt. II. *Biometrika*, XXXVIII (June, 1951), 159.

[35]M. L. Burnstein, "The Demand for Household Refrigeration in the United States," Part III in Arnold C. Harberger (ed.), *The Demand for Durable Goods* (Chicago: University of Chicago Press, 1960), p. 100.

w_{t-1} and thus D_{t-1} and w_t are correlated, because D_t and w_t are correlated. This assumption is valid in most economic time series data—conventionally time series data are assumed to be generated by the linear first order difference equation, especially since Orcutt's study.[36] That is, least-square principles may not be directly applicable in certain cases and may require augmented and modified principles, e.g., the generalized least-square model.

The causes of the biases found in the results of (8) require further elaboration. First, according to the pioneering study of Orcutt and Cochrane's Monte Carlo work with twenty random samples, [37] in the first order autoregressive scheme

$$x_t = 0.4x_{t-1} + u_t$$

where the u_t is positively autocorrelated and approximately three times as large in magnitude as x, the results showed 0.90 as the estimated coefficient with a 0.02 standard error, i.e., $2\frac{1}{4}$ times of the true value 0.4. Second, autocorrelated disturbance alone does not yield biased estimates, but lagged variables also yield a bias; however, the joint result cannot be inferred as the simple addition of their separate results. In addition, the estimated t and F values are biased. Subsequently, the Durbin-Watson coefficient is asymptotically biased toward two.[38] As a matter of fact, usefulness of the Durbin-Watson statistics is properly limited by their famous study that places restrictions on their statistical results which "they . . . do not apply to their autoregressive scheme and similar models in which the lagged values of the dependent variable occur as independent variables."[39]

A treatment of bias in standard errors has been pioneered by Professor

---

[36]G. Orcutt, "A Study of Autoregressive Nature of the Time Series Used for Tinbergen's Model of the Economic System of the United States, 1919–1932."

[37]G. H. Orcutt and D. Cochrane, "A Sampling Study of the Merits of Autoregressive and Reduced Form Transformations in Regression Analysis," *Journal of American Statistical Association*, XLIV (March, 1949), 356–72, particularly p. 365.

Cf. A more complicated study is done by E. Malinvaud who develops a model containing a lagged endogenous variable, exogenous variable, and a constant term with 20 random samples. The results are summarized in his *Statistical Methods of Econometrics* (Chicago: Rand McNally & Co., 1966), pp. 455–56.

[38]See Griliches' "A Note on Serial Correlation Bias in Estimates of Distributed Lags;" also Marc Nerlove and Kenneth F. Wallis, "Use of the Durbin-Watson Statistics in Inappropriate Situation," *Econometrica*, XXXIV (January, 1966), 235–38.

[39]Durbin and Watson, "Testing for Serial Correlation in Least-Squares Regression," p. 159.

Wold[40] and subsequently advanced by Zellner.[41] Zellner corrects the standard errors of the Haavelmo classical work by accounting for temporal dependence of the stochastic terms.[42] Lyttkens[43] further develops the Wold-Zellner scheme at Wold's suggestion in cases where inclusion of lagged endogenous variables among regressors and autocorrelation between residuals occur at the same time due to an incomplete model specification.

Thus according to Lyttkens, if a model is expressed as

$$Y_t = b_i Z_{it} + U_t \ (i = 1,2,\ldots; t = 1,2,\ldots,T)$$

$$U_t = r_j U_{t-j} + v_t \ (j = 1,2,\ldots)$$

where $/r_j/ < 1$; $E(v_t) = 0$ and $E(v_t v_{t+s}) = \sigma^2$ if $s = 0$

$$= 0 \text{ if } s \neq 0 \text{ for all } t.$$

Y is the endogenous variable; Z_i represents the exogenous and lagged endogenous variables. For convenience, variables are assumed to be measured from their mean values to eliminate the intercept.

Lyttkens' formula (actually a modification of Wold-Zellner's) for the above scheme is:

$$d(b_i) \simeq (S_u/S_{zi})\,(T^{-\frac{1}{2}})F \text{ and } L = (\ddot{b}_i - b_i)/d(b_i)$$

$$F = (1 + 2r_i p_i + 2R_k R_{-k})^{\frac{1}{2}} \quad k = 1,2,\ldots$$

where $d(b)$ denotes the standard error of the regression coefficient; S_u and S_{zi} are the observed standard deviations of U and Z_i, respectively; L is a significant criterion; $\ddot{b}_i$ is the calculated coefficient of b_i; F can be termed the Wold-Zellner-Lyttkens correction factor for the standard error of the regression coefficient; R_k and R_{-k} are two sets of correlation coefficients between the regressor and future residuals and the past residuals, respectively. For example, if the residuals are assumed as the first order autoregressive scheme, the Wold-Zellner-Lyttkens correction

---

[40]See Professor Herman Wold's path-breaking work in this area, "On Least-Square Regression with Autocorrelated Variables and Residuals," *Bulletin de l' Institut International Statistique*, XXXII (1950), 290–94; also see his *Demand Analysis: A Study in Econometrics* (New York; John Wiley & Sons, 1953 and Stockholm: Almzvist & Wiksell, 1952), pp. 209–13. Actual application can be found on p. 236.

[41]Arnold Zellner, "Econometric Estimation with Temporally Dependent Disturbance Terms," *International Economic Review*, II (May, 1961), 164–78.

[42]The standard errors are almost twice as large as Haavelmo's classical results. See *Ibid.*

[43]Ejnar Lyttkens, "Standard Errors of Regression Coefficients by Autocorrelated Residuals," in Herman Wold (ed), *Econometric Model Building* (Amsterdam: North-Holland Publishing Co., 1964), pp. 169–228.

factor

$$F = (1 + 2r_1 p_1 + 2R_1 R_{-1})^{\frac{1}{2}}$$

A correction of bias from the standard errors is more crucial than any other, because standard errors must be made unbiased in order to produce prediction accuracy and, subsequently, a policy implication.

Next, it may be intuitively argued that the serial correlation of the residuals is due to the distributed lags, by comparing the results of (8) with the following:

$$(9) \quad D_t = -3.7972 + 1.1927Y_t + 0.5426P_t$$
$$\qquad (1.7336) \quad (.2398) \quad (1.3347)$$

$R^2 = .8783$
$SEE = .0221$
$F = 45.63$
$DW = .73$

On the other hand, according to Griliches, the results of (9) are not evidence of a distributed lag model.[44] Furthermore, the distributed lag bias becomes weaker for yearly data.[45] Accordingly, it shall be postulated only to indicate the direction of bias that the coefficients of (8) are biased upward particularly for the coefficient of D_{t-1}. Second, it shall be assumed that if the bias in the estimated Durbin-Watson coefficient 2.48 in (8) is within the range of 0.66, a correction of the bias will be insignificant and will remain within the same inconclusive boundary of serial correlation (0.86 is the lower boundary at 5% significance level). This tentative speculation is based on calculations of the parameters of (8), (8a), and (9) by the rational and convincing Taylor-Wilson-Houthakker "Three-Pass Least Squares" method.[46] In addition, the speculations are analyzed against various two-stage tests of the samples, such as the Durbin method, Cochrane-Orcutt suggested successive difference method,[47] and Rao-

[44]Griliches, "A Note on Serial Correlation Bias on Serial Correlation Bias in Estimates of Distributed Lags," p. 71.

[45]Michael K. Evans, *Macroeconomic Activity: Theory, Forecasting, and Control: An Econometric Approach* (New York: Harper & Row, 1969), p. 53.

[46]Lester D. Taylor and Thomas A. Wilson, "Three-Pass Least Squares: A Method for Estimating Models with a Lagged Dependent Variable," *Review of Economics and Statistics*, XLVI (November, 1964), 329–46 and Houthakker and Taylor, *Consumer Demand.*

[47]J. Durbin, "Estimation of Parameters in Time-Series Regression Models," *Journal of Royal Statistical Society*, Series B, XXII (January, 1960), 139–53 and his "A Sampling Study of the Merits of Autoregressive . . ."

Griliches two-stage regression method.[48] Actually, all of the above methods introduced more serious new bias, instead of eliminating original bias, perhaps due to an insignificant calculated value of the first order autoregressive coefficient from calculated residuals of tin-can models.

In addition, it is proved to be incorrect to apply these methods to eliminate possible bias, unless the true value of the first order autoregressive coefficient (r_1) is higher than some critical value (say 0.4 in Rao-Griliches').[49] And, contrary to popular belief, if there is negative autocorrelation as in the tin-can model, these "two and three stage methods" of eliminating biases are put in doubt.[50] These limitations are due to the introduction of new biases in the process of eliminating old biases. Conceivably, this is the case of the tin-can industry's time series data, 1950–1966.

At this point, it is important to point out Taylor-Wilson-Houthakker's Monte Carlo study which initiated the "three-pass least squares" method and their subsequent empirical work. The latter study tried to determine the better method between the three-pass least squares and ordinary least-squares method. This attempt is the most comprehensive study since Henry Schultz' classical work in the 1930s of U.S. consumption. In their work, sixty-one consumption categories are estimated by the ordinary least-squares method in which the Durbin-Watson coefficients are more than the lower boundary. Second, twenty-three categories are estimated by the three-pass least squares method in which the Durbin-Watson coefficients are around or lower than the lower boundary.

From these studies, (i.e., Taylor-Wilson's findings, from their Monte Carlo study; Houthakker-Taylor's practical approach which attempted to eliminate any new biases and correct old biases; and the negative autocorrelation consideration), it can be concluded that result (8) is as fairly good as an approximation of the tin-can demand relation as the results of the ID- and CC-systems.

In concluding these remarks on the inherent biases in the time-series data, there are in reality many other biases, notable among which are: Hurwiz' small sample bias,[51] errors of observation and measurement,

---

[48]Potluri Rao and Ziv Griliches, "Small-Sample Properties of Several Two-Stage Regression Methods in the Context of Auto-correlated Errors," *Journal of American Statistical Association*, LXIV (March, 1969), 253–72.

[49]*Ibid.*, p. 263

[50]See an interesting argument by Houthakker and Taylor, *Consumer Demand in the United States, 1929–1970*, P. 49 and its footnote, commenting on the Malinvaud finding.

[51]Leonid Hurwicz, "Least Squares Bias in Time Series," in T. C. Koopmans (ed.), *Statistical Inference in Dynamic Economic Models*, Cowles Commission Monograph 10 (New York: John Wiley & Sons, 1950), pp. 365–83.

particularly in the explanatory variables, and the assumptions simulated from the analysis of controllable data. In addition, problems of multicollinearity and complicated heteroscedasticity are usually compounded by economic time-series analysis. A treatment of these problems, however, is beyond the scope of this comparative structural study. In the words of J. Johnston:

> Unfortunately, the present stage of development of the subejct might be likened to a primitive stage in medicine where a doctor is able to treat only *one* complaint at a time. . . . if both problems arise simultaneously, we cannot treat them by somewhat adding together the treatments appropriate for the cases in isolation; instead, we require a properly developed, integrated treatment, designed for the case at hand, but this is not yet available.[52]

b. The Circular-Chain System

A simple circular chain system for the U.S. tin-can industry is constructed as similarly as possible to the ID- and CC-systems as well as the bicausal-chain system. This construction disregards a priori information on relative exogeniety and price rigidity of tin-cans, solely for comparative purposes.

(1) $S = a_0 + a_1 R_{-1} + a_2 TP + a_3 P_{-1} + u_1$ (Supply)

(2) $P = b_0 + b_1 Y + b_2 D + b_3 T + u_2$ (Demand)

(3) $S = D = Q$ (Equilibrium Assumption)

The supply relation (1) is exactly the same as in the CC-system as well as in the bicausal chain system. Of course, as in the bicausal chain system, the current price variable P can be employed instead of the lagged price variable P_{-1} in (1) because of the a priori information on tin-can prices.

The rationality of the circular chain model is the same as in the bicausal

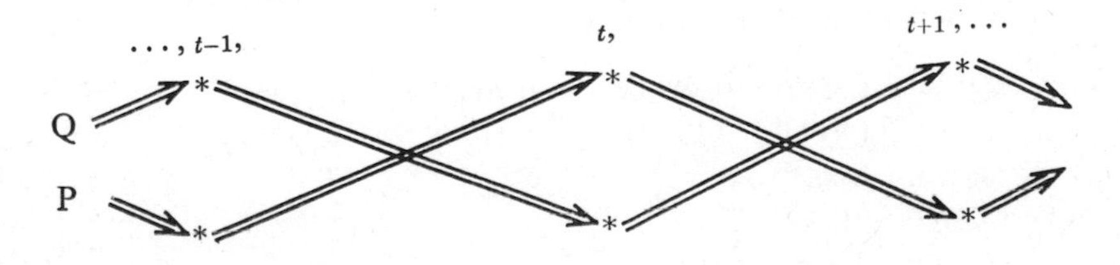

[52]J. Johnston, *Econometric Methods* (New York: McGrawHill, 1963), p. 147.

chain system. The difference is the causal specification of the demand relation (2), i.e., the position of D and P are interchanged. An arrow scheme specification of the system thus yields as in the above figure. As was done before, the influences of the exogenous variables are not shown in the figure for simplicity in drawing.

As has been indicated before, the arrows in the arrow scheme indicate a flow of causation among the current and lagged endogenous variables. The coefficient matrix of the endogenous variables in the circular chain system is,

$$\begin{bmatrix} 1 & 0 \\ -b_2 & -1 \end{bmatrix}$$

Consequently, this model has the formal property of the ID-system. However, (2) can be re-specified in terms of conditional expectations if this author's corollary to theorem 1 is an adequate one.

$$(4) \qquad E(Q^s/R_{-1},TP,P_{-1}) = a_o + a_1R_{-1} + a_2TP + a_3P_{-1}$$

$$(5) \qquad E(P/Y,Q^d,T) = b_o + b_1Y + b_2Q + b_3T$$

Of course, the specification of supply relation (4) is exactly the same as in the bicausal chain system.

Remarks.—It can be easily recognized that demand relation (2), and subsequently the specification of (5) are not adequate ones for the tin-can industry; however, this consequence is strictly the result of explaining the competing models through comparative models. As has been stated in the discussion of characteristics of the tin-can industry in the previous section B, tin-can prices are determined by the giant oligopolists' decision-making processes rather than by market forces at least in the short-run. And also, it has been empirically confirmed that the price variable is more exogenous than endogenous in this highly concentrated industry. Therefore, the demand relation (2) is a misspecification of the relation but is deliberately done solely for the purpose of practical operation of the circular chain system.

The results of the system are:

$$(6) \qquad Q^s = \underset{(.9193)}{-1.3287} + \underset{(.0757)}{0.3990R_{-1}} - \underset{(.4196)}{0.7097TP} + \underset{(.3725)}{0.2740P}$$

$R^2 = .9386$
$SEE = .0163$
$F = 61.12$
$DW = 1.84$

$$(7) \quad P = \underset{(.1964)}{1.3219} + \underset{(.0810)}{0.0901Y} + \underset{(.1171)}{0.1400D} - \underset{(.0149)}{0.0169T}$$

$R^2 = .7240$
$SEE = .0045$
$F = 10.49$
$DW = .92$

When (7) is compared with (7) in the bicausal chain system, the inadequate specification of the demand relation of the circular chain system is evident and the result confirms the a priori information on the characteristics of tin-can prices.

In addition, if the calculated values of Q^s from (6) is substituted for D in (7), the results are more discouraging,

$$(7\text{–a}) \quad P = \underset{(.2021)}{1.2321} + \underset{(.0759)}{0.1562Y} + \underset{(.0855)}{0.0045\ddot{Q}^s} - \underset{(.0114)}{0.0018T}$$

where $\ddot{Q}^s$ denotes the calculated values from (6)

$R^2 = .6912$
$SEE = .0048$
$F = 8.95$
$DW = .7707$

But as earlier expected, the circular chain specification of the tin-can industry is inadequate. As a result, it is not necessary to evaluate the demand relation of the circular chain system further.

Table 2

Summary of Parameters and Statistics of the Four Systems

		Supply						
		R_{-1}	TP	P	P_{-1}	R^2	SEE	DW*
ID		0.1231 (.0869)	−0.8397 (.3010)	3.5775 (1.2180)		.9626	.0127	2.09
CC or CCID	A	0.2328 (.0714)	−0.6858 (.3161)	1.6461 (.7313)		.9549	.0140	1.84
	B	0.3009 (.0757)	−0.7097 (.4196)		0.2740 (.3725)	.9386	.0163	1.41
		Demand						
		Y	P	T	D_{-1}			
ID		0.5460 (.4426)	−0.3582 (2.6339)	0.1109 (.0180)		.9709	.0111	2.32

CC	0.6526	−1.1455	0.1122		.9714	.0110	2.17
	(.3631)	(2.3476)	(.0175)				
Bicausal Chain	0.5157	−0.9723		0.7244	.9439	.0154	2.49
	(.2434)	(1.0123)		(.1891)			
	Price						
	Y	TP	R_{-1}	T			
ID	0.2622	−0.1279	−0.0445	−0.0053	.7111	0.048	0.84
	(.1376)	(.2241)	(.0511)	(.0173)			
	Y	$(D_{-1}-\ddot{S})$					
CC	0.1434	0.1785			.8174	.0035	1.36
	(.0214)	(.0593)					
	Y	D	T				
Circular Chain	0.0901	0.1400	−0.0169		.7240	.0045	0.92
	(.0810)	(.1171)	(.0149)				

Notes: *Cases A and B for the supply in CC- or CCID-systems indicates employment of P_t or P_{t-1} as explanatory variables, respectively.*

*The lower and upper bounds for 16 observations with three independent variables are 0.86–1.73 at 5% significance level, 0.75–1.59 at 2.5% level, and 0.63–1.44 at 1% level, respectively; and the Theil-Nagar statistic is 1.53 at 5% significance level and 1.24 at 1% level, respectively: These bounds with two independent variables are 0.98–1.54; and the Theil-Nagar's are 1.37 at 5% and 1.08 at 1% significance level.

4. A Summary Evaluation

A summary evaluation of the alternative empirical results for the tin-can industry, 1950–1966, is presented in light of the a priori theory in order of (A) the supply relation, (B) the demand relation, and (C) the price relation. Although an evaluation of the dynamic and predictive powers of each system might be appropriate here, it will be postponed for later discussion in conjunction with a summary of the theoretical arguments in previous chapters, in order to prevent overlapping with the concluding chapter.

a. The Supply Relation

The a priori theory is best confirmed by case *A* of the CC- and CCID-systems; by case *B* in which the coefficient of R_{-1} is more properly, expressed in terms of its magnitude and standard error. The price elasticity however, is too large in magnitude to rely on, particularly in the ID-system. The other three systems' elasticity are also very high but its magnitude is less than half of the ID-system.

All four systems have measures of "goodness of fit" and the standard errors shown are asymptotic, except for coefficient of R_{-1} in the ID-system and that of *TP* and P_{-1} in case *B*. Furthermore, for the ID-system and case *A* of the CC- or CCID-system, we can accept the null hypothesis of autocorrelation at the 5% significance level. For case *B*, the Durbin-Watson coefficient indicates an inconclusive region, but is conclusive in terms of the Theil-Nagar statistic by which the null hypothesis can be accepted at the 1% significance level. The supply relation of case *A* of the CC- and CCID-system provides quite satisfactory information, regardless of the model's simplicity.

b. The Demand Relation

All four systems, except the circular chain system, have measures of "goodness of fit" for the demand relation as a whole. Unfortunately, no system has an asymptotic standard error for the price elasticity, regardless of its proper sign. The elasticity magnitude of the ID-system appears to be the most satisfactory because of its low elasticity. This qualification, however, also generates ample doubt in terms of the standard error. This standard error is more than seven times its price elasticity, and the standard error of income elasticity is almost the same as the price elasticity. The *DW* coefficient has an inconclusive boundary but is significant at the 5% level in terms of the Theil-Nagar statistic.

In contrast, the CC-system's price elasticity is very high as a producer's good, because the standard error is almost twice the elasticity which, however, is much smaller than that of the ID-system. Income elasticity is generally good but is just short of the asymptotic level. The *DW* coefficient confirms the null-hypothesis of autocorrelation at the 5% significance level.

It is not surprising, however, to gain better results from the bicausal chain system, which derives an asymptotic level for the standard error of income elasticity and the lowest magnitude of standard error for price elasticity (even if the standard error does not indicate an asymptotic level.) The significant finding by this system is that the Houthakker-Taylor "habit formation theory" is realized in the relations of canned good consumption, regardless of possible serious biases due to the inclusion of the lagged dependent variable.[53] Although Wod-Lyttkens-Zellner's correction factor for the standard error as well as Griliches' bias factor for the *DW* coefficient are speculated, the system may be superior to the other systems. This comparative conclusion concurs with the Houthakker-Taylor study, in which demand relations are presented without modification provided that the *DW* coefficient is above the lower boundary of the inconclusive region.[54] In this case, the *DW* coefficient 2.48 is not far from the upper boundary of 2.27, i.e., 0.21 short of accepting the null hypothesis at the 5% significance level, but can be accepted at the 5% significance level in terms of the Theil-Nagar statistic.

c. The Price Relation

This author is quite satisfied with the performance of the Woldian price mechanism because the price relation is one of the most delicate relations in the empirical study. As has been presented in detail, the Woldian approach is initiated by an implementation of disequilibrium processes and is based on *A*. Cournot's verbal explanation of the forces of price movements in competitive agricultural markets. Although the tin-can industry is structured as a "quasi-duopoly" the price mechanism yields fairly satisfactory information. The standard error of coefficients of the price relation are asymptotic and the *DW* coefficient justifies the null hypothesis of autocorrelation in terms of the Theil-Nagar statistic far above the 1% level but 0.01 short of the 5% level.

In retrospect and as explained above, the circular chain system is inappropriate for this particular industry, due to the relative exogeneity a priori and the a posteriori of the price variable. In addition the reduced form of the ID-system has no economic meaning and is only useful as a tool for prediction of endogenous variables. This prediction equation is important and will be presented in the following concluding chapter.

---

[53]See "Some Remarks . . ." above, pp. 130–35.
[54]See *ibid.*

CHAPTER VII

SUMMARY AND CONCLUDING REMARKS

CHAPTER VII

SUMMARY AND CONCLUDING REMARKS

It is quite natural to have diversified views of econometric model-building for available time series data. Econometric models are abstracted and approximated from the real world by limiting the number of variables in each relation and in the system as a whole. The number of relations in the system is also limited in order to construct an empirically feasible model. Prior to approximation, the most essential decision, therefore, must be made to determine whether the real world will be perceived as one of interdependency or recursivity.

Models based on interdependence invalidate the technique of single equation least-square estimation. This invalidation is primarily due to three reasons: first, the earlier arguments on the "choice-of-regression" ; second, the implementation of Walras-Keynes' equilibrium or moving equilibrium assumption in a system; and finally, the availability of only aggregated data in terms of a theoretical industry and/or in terms of long time spans. In contrast Wold's economic model perceives the world as approximately recursive due to the following reasons: first, each autonomous economic behaving unit acts in accordance with its own goal, and therefore, in reality, market processes behave more similarly to Lundberg-Lindahl's disequilibrium process than to an equilibrium one; second, the disequilibrium process, which begins with each behaving unit's expectations, is fundamentally dynamic and derives its driving forces from the gap between its expectation and realization; finally, the disequilibrium process therefore should explain approximate direction of movement even with aggregated time series data.

Thus, the two opposing views of the real world have created different systems of simultaneous equations. The latter view of recursivity incorporates causality as the instrumentality of processes other than the metaphysical "Principle of Causality"[1] and is specified as a completely decomposable triangular matrix of endogenous variables. On the other hand, the prior view of interdependency is described as an indecomposable block matrix.

Accepting the interdependent (ID) system as an all-purpose structural model, the ID-researchers have opened many path-breaking avenues for modern econometric techniques and theories. However, the ID-approach has been unable to establish its intended role in structural model-building, contrary to the higher aspiration level of its originators. As stated earlier, there are some crucial theoretical dilemmas and problems inherent in the ID-system concerning economic and stochastic theories. Consequently, the results of this empirical study have been disappointing for the ID-system. "The concrete results of our (the ID-researchers) efforts and quantitative measurement often seem to get worse the more refinement of tools and logical stringency we call into play; "[2] however, the ID-system has been "oversold . . . (and) . . . extravagent claims have been made or implied that something was 'wrong' or 'incorrect' with all previous empirical studies in econometrics, that the great pioneering efforts of such people as Schultz (statistical demand curve), Douglas (statistical production functions) and Tinbergen (statistical business cycle models) would all have to be redone and put right. "[3]

As a result, the causal chain (CC) system was introduced into this study in order to probe in depth a possible alternative approach to the dilemma inherent in the ID-system. This attempt was conducted in spite of the fact that the ID-protagonists had ruled out the CC-system as a "biased least squares method." According to our data, the CC-system can be demonstrated as theoretically superior to the ID-system. When a structural model was specified by the Tinbergen-Wold unidirectional arrow

---

[1]However, this is not to deny the possibility of causal inference—for example, to calculate a position of the Moon by inspecting the tidal water movements, one can conclude that the Moon is the cause of the tidal movements although not conversely.

[2]Trygve Haavelmo, "The Role of the Econometrician in the Advancement of Economic Theory," *Econometrica*, XXVI (July, 1958), 355.

[3]L. R. Klein, "Single Equation vs. Equation System Methods of Estimation in Econometrics," *Econometrica*, XXVIII (October, 1960), 855–65.

scheme, which is based on the disequilibrium dynamic process, no dilemmas occurred as in the ID-system. In short, we found in theory that the CC-system was much more than an alternative to the ID-system, contrary to our original intuitive speculation that the former was an alternative to the latter in certain cases.

If the above is true, why do many ID-protagonists rule out the CC-system? First, their overall concept of the CC-system is incorrect and they misunderstand the meaning of the term "causality" in light of metaphysics. In most cases, therefore, the ID-protagonists have mislabeled certain models as CC-systems or recursive-systems, without providing necessary theoretical qualifications. Specifically, it is deceptive to term a single equation model as a CC-system without providing proper qualifications (e.g., the Wold Proximity Theorem). It is wrong to define a system of simultaneous equations as a CC-system without providing disequilibrium conditions and without providing for the implementation of causality through an arrow scheme specification of the system. Also it is misleading to present the strict vector regression system of simultaneous equations as the typical CC-system because the former is only the theoretical result of a special case of the CC-system. In a footnote, it has been pointed out that the ID-system is an extreme generalization of the vector regression system, and results in an unspecifiable direction for the arrow scheme, i.e., non-unidirectional.

Second, due to this misconception of the CC-system, the ID-advocates have confused the means and ends of the CC-system. For example, when they present a comparative study in order to condemn the CC-system or in order to support the ID-system, they are almost exclusively critical of the least-squares methodology (means) of the CC-system as if the means were the ends of the system—thus failing to consider the full model of the CC-system. As a result, the ID-protagonists have advanced great contributions through many sophisticated estimation techniques, particularly through many Monte Carlo studies with small samples. Unfortunately, because their work has been based mainly upon an extreme conjecture on interdependency, their results have been insufficient and irrational in comparison to the end results of the CC-system.

Although enormous efforts have been conducted to invent alternate estimation techniques, all techniques of the ID-system have been concerned with the overidentified case in general as if it were an absolute formal property of the real world. As a result, it has been difficult to find an acceptable rationalization why a structural model should always be overidentified. Liu's arguments exemplify the predominance of unacceptable rationalizations which assert that the real world is always more simultaneous than investigators think and therefore the world is truly underidentified.[4] But if this conjecture is true, existing ID-school estimation techniques would lose much of their utility. However, for the first time, a rational counterargument has been presented by Professor Fisher[5] in terms of a generalization of Wold's Proximity Theorem, and has led to the construction of the *Brookings Quarterly Econometric Model.*[6]

Even this effort, however, does not completely prove the adequacy of the ID-system because it still retains several dilemmas. These dilemmas are partly due to a spherical transformation of parameters into diffrent dimentional space and due to an emphasis on reduced forms. Perhaps, these problems cannot be solved without re-examining their extreme conjecture; although, it should be pointed out that many dilemmas have been partially solved by the well-known Theil two-stage least-squares method and Basmann's analogous method, giving some emphasis to the structural parameters. However, these successes are by-products of estimation methodology rather than a direct attack on the problems through a rational model.

In contrast, as has been mentioned above, the CC-system does not have the dilemmas found in the ID-system, regardless of the former's heavy dependence on the basic theorem on least-squares. Of course, the unidirectional arrow scheme specification of the structural model calls for the least-squares technique but not vice versa. The CC-system appears to be a mathematically inflexible triangle, but contrary to this formality, the triangle is a theoretical criterion for an adequate dynamic disequilibrium model specification, so as to implement a direction of movements. When it is impossible to adopt a triangular model specification in constructing the CC-system, it is legitimate to substitute the block matrix as an approximation of the triangular model. However, this substitution should not be conceived as a mutual interdependency and should be augmented by a subjective causal interpretation of the system through an arrow scheme specification—the causalized interdependent (CCID) system.

The CCID-system is classified as a generalization of the vector regres-

---

[4]Ta-Chung Liu, "A Simple Forecasting Model for the U.S. Economy," *International Monetary Fund: Staff Papers*, IV (August, 1955), 436–66 and his "Underidentification, Structural Estimation, and Forecasting," *Econometrica*, XXVIII (October, 1960), 855–65.

[5]Franklin M. Fisher, "On the Cost of Approximate Specification in Simultaneous Equation Estimation," *Econometrica*, XXXIX (April, 1961), 139–70.

[6]Franklin M. Fisher, "Dynamic Structure and Estimation in Economy-Wide Econometric Models," *The Brookings Quarterly Econometric Model of the United States*, ed. by J. S. Duesenberry *et al.* (Chicago: Rand McNally & Company, 1965), pp. 589–635.

sion system, in which a block matrix of coefficients of endogenous variables is indigenous as in the ID-system. Through a unidirectional arrow scheme specification of the model, the CCID-system can be subclassified as bi-causal chain and circular chain systems. As a result, the CCID-system supports the feasibility of empirical testing as an approximation of the CC-system if the triangular matrix formation cannot be adopted. Pragmatically, this process of empirical testing is much better than the alternative of nothing, even if it is only an approximation of the CC-system.

Thus, the CCID-system is distinctively different from the ID-system in the development of the structural form, in spite of identical formal appearances. In operation, the CCID-system's structural form is practically the same as in the CC-system but quite unlike that in the ID-system. The ID-system utilizes the structural form as a theoretical tool to derive the reduced form for prediction. Consequently, the locus of the dilemma in the ID-system occurs in the explicit use of the structural form; whereas, the locus of the dilemma in the CCID-system occurs in the explicit use of the reduced form. This difference exists because of the stochastic non-equivalence between the structural form and the reduced form of the two systems. On the other hand, the CC-system exhibits neither dilemma due to Wold's chain of iterative substitution by which the structural form and the reduced form are proved to be isomorphous, algebraically and stochastically.

Third, there are many comparisons coefficient-by-coefficient between various ID-estimation techniques and the simple least-square estimates. All these comparisons by the ID-school, however, are unfairly biased in favor of the ID-system. They build a typical ID-model (which is the same as producing poor estimates by the least-squares method); apply their various estimating techniques; and compare the results. This methodology is unacceptable as a rational comparative technique, although it does reaffirm once again the well-known built-in Haavelmo classical bias. According to our definition of the CC-system, the comparisons ill-fit the ID- and CC-systems.

In spite of the biased use of the least-squares method by these comparative studies, it seems to be a general concensus today that the direct application of the least-squares method to structural equations, *seriatim*, yields a good estimate in many cases regardless of built-in biases; moreover, in many instances the method yields superior estimation results, e.g., in agricultural demand relations.[7] Furthermore, according to Profes-

[7]See for example, Karl A. Fox, "Structural Analysis and the Measurement of Demand for Farm Products," *Review of Economics and Statistics*, XXXVII (February, 1954), 57–66.

sor Klein's recent intensive study,[8] even for the heavily aggregated interdependent macro-economic model with annual data, the least-squares method generally yields far better results than the classical limited-information maximum likelihood method, and results almost equal to the two stage least-squares method and the full-information maximum likelihood method. According to most empirical research, the major failure of the ID-system has occurred in international trade and cross-sectional relationships.[9] Such results indirectly demonstrate the wrong conjecture regarding the mutual-interdependency of the real world and, in turn, suggest the recursivity of the real world.

Accordingly, past chapters have argued that the Haavelmo bias is true when the least-squares method is applied directly to structural relations of the ID-system; however, the bias is so small compared with other inherent biases in time series data. Therefore, it would be delusory to correct the bias and it is quite possible that more serious new biases will be introduced in the process of eliminating old ones. This conclusion is based on the dilemmas of the ID-system in addition to cummulative sensitivity in multicollinearity and autocorrelation in the process of dimentional spherical transformations both ways.

These pessimistic findings regarding the ID-system and the beauty of the least-squares theorem are not surprising results if one truly understands Wold's underlying motivation in initiating his powerful Proximity Theorem as well as this author's corollaries to the theorem. Thus, in spite of the fact that the selection of an estimation technique is in general non-controversial after a model is specified, the ID-protagonists have applied the least-squares method to the relations of the ID-system to discredit the CC-system in terms of a goodness-of-fit. Clearly, these comparative studies have been biased in favor of the ID-system from the beginning, and they cannot claim to be objective comparative studies of the ID- and CC-systems. Therefore, these studies have value only as mental exercises for beginning students in their attempts to prove the classical Haavelmo bias when the least-squares method is applied directly to the ID-system.

As a consequence, it was necessary to conduct our own case study to establish a true comparative study of the alternative systems. Because it was found that the CC-system was more realistic and rational, at least

---

[8] L. R. Klein, "Problems in the Estimation of Interdependent Systems," in *Model Building in the Human Sciences*, ed. by Herman O. A. Wold (Monaco: Union Europeenne D'Edition, 1966), pp. 52–87.

[9] See for example, S. J. Prais, "Econometric Research in International Trade: Review," *Kyklos*, IV (1962), 560–79.

in its theoretical aspects, than the ID-system and because it had more correct views of the real world—recursivity—this study began its model construction with the ID-system, which is theoretically weaker than the CC-system. First a preliminary test run was conducted to yield reasonable empirical results for the ID-system and subsequently other systems were constructed as similarly as possible to the ID-system. As was mentioned in the preceding chapter, this section will present the significant findings of our previous theoretical arguments. In addition, empirical results of the tin-can industry will be listed to illustrate the attributes of the alternative systems in order to emphasize the aim of this study.

A. CONJECTURE ON DYNAMICS

Assuming the real world to be approximately recursive, we considered the dynamic property of the CC-system. If this viewpoint of recursivity is more correct than others, it becomes an interesting point to consider the dynamic property of the tin-can industry, particularly its price mechanism which is in line with the dynamization of Cournot's verbal argument in his *Research*. It was argued that the characteristics of the ID-system in relation to the tin-can industry were due to a static equilibrium assumption between market demand and supply; whereas, those of the CC-system were due to explicit implementation of a disequilibrium reality (asymmetry) between demand and supply which were never equal regardless of modern industrial planning systems.

Referring to the preceding chapter for convenience, if the supply relation (4) and the demand relation (6) in the CC-system replaced price mechanism (5), the following difference equation is obtained:

$$(1) \qquad P_t + 0.0583P_{t-1} = L_{cc}$$

where L_{cc} stands for a linear combination of the values of the remaining variables including their intercepts in the system as a constant.

If a moving price equilibrium (say, P_e) is defined as,

$$(2) \qquad P_t = P_{t-1} = P_e$$

thus,

$$(3) \qquad P_e + 0.0583P_e = L_{cc}$$

and then (1) minus (3) will yield

$$(4) \qquad P_t^* + 0.0583P_{t-1}^* = 0$$

where $P_t^* = P_t - P_e$ and $0.0583P_{t-1}^* = 0.0583(P_{t-1} - P_e)$.
Therefore, the solution of (4) is

$$(5) \qquad P_t^* = P_o^* (-0.0583)^t$$

where P_o^* is the deviation of the market price from its equilibrium price at some prescribed initial time, zero.

Accordingly, the behavior of the solution sequence $\{P_t^*\}$ converges with heavily damped oscillation toward the equilibrium price, *centeris paribus.* Its relative speed of convergence is mainly influenced by the value of c_2 in relation (3) of the CC-system—(the stock adjustment coefficient) in the price mechanism. The results are exactly in conformity with our theoretical argument that the disequilibrium (asymmetry) brings convergence toward rather than divergence from equilibrium.

In the bicausal chain system, the supply relation (the same as the CC-systems) is set as equal to the demand relation based on its equilibrium assumption. Then as was developed above, we derive

$$(7) \qquad P_t = P_{t-1} = P_e$$

$$(8) \qquad P_t^* = P_o^* (-0.2818)^t$$

where notational meaning remains the same as the above. As in the CC-system, the behavior of the solution sequence $\{P_t^*\}$ rapidly converges toward the equilibrium price, *ceteris paribus.*

For comparative purposes, it is necessary to modify the ID-system in order to find a dynamic property of the price mechanism of the market in line with the above development. In doing so, P_t in the supply relation of the ID-system in the preceding chapter is replaced by P_{t-1}. This revision of the system, however, does not give any disadvantage to the system because of the following results. Due to the revision, the supply relation can be estimated by the least-squares method which yields results exactly the same as in the alternative systems. For the demand relation, the calculated values of the price ($\ddot{P}$) is employed in place of the price variable in that relation. (The calculated values of the price is derived, reducing the price on R_{-1}, Y, TP, P_{-1} and T.)

The results are:

$$(9) \qquad D_t = \underset{(.0113)}{-0.0002} + \underset{(.1837)}{0.4486Y_t} - \underset{(.3348)}{0.3115\ddot{P}_t} + \underset{(.0171)}{0.1208T}$$

$$R^2 = .9984$$
$$DW = 2.29$$

Subsequently, in the same manner as the alternative systems, the revised supply relation and (9) are postulated in an equilibrium condition.

(10) $$P_t = -0.8796P_{t-1} + L_{ID}$$

where L_{ID} stands for a linear combination of the values of the remaining variables including intercepts in the system.

If P_e is assumed as a moving price equilibrium value as in the alternative systems,

(11) $$P_t = P_{t-1} = P_e$$

Therefore,

(12) $$P_t^* = P_o^* (-0.8796)^t$$

where the notational meaning remains the same as the alternative systems. Hence, clearly, the price will oscillate convergently toward the equilibrium price, *ceteris paribus*.

In retrospect, all three systems performed well in conformance with the well-known market mechanism. The differences in dampness and amplitude of their oscillation are a matter of degree rather than of kind; however, the oscillation and amplitude of the ID-system is largest and that of the CC-system is the smallest, i.e., (ID = /0.8796/)>(*BC* = /0.2818/)>(*CC*=/0.0583/). This result demonstrates that asymmetry tends to create more stability than does symmetry and justifies our theoretical argument. It has been argued that disequilibrium describes reality and that equilibrium is only an approximation of disequilibrium because the former is a special case of disequilibrium. In addition the statistical results confirm the fact that the CCID-system has a more dynamic property than the ID-system regardless of the CCID-system's equilibrium assumption being the same as that of the ID-system in this case study.

B. EX-POST AND EX-ANTE PREDICTIONS OF THE ALTERNATIVE SYSTEMS

The following ex-post and ex-ante predictions of the alternative systems are presented in light of Theil's Inequality Coefficient[10] (hereafter, simply

[10]Henri Theil, *Economic Forecasts and Policy* (2nd rev. ed.; Amsterdam: North-Holland Publishing Company, 1961.), pp. 31–48.

Actually, it may be better to use the Gadd-Wold Janus Quotient than Theil's Inequali-

referred to as Theil's) in lieu of a complicated graphic method. However, it shall be noted that an ex-ante prediction cannot have much utility for this comparative study, regardless of its utmost importance in policy implication. The reason is that a true sense of ex-ante forecasting should be done by projecting exogenous variables through adequate ancillary

Table 3

The Measure of Prediction Accuracy for the Observation Range Expressed by Theil's Inequality Coefficient

Supply		Demand		Price	
ID-(5)	.004,23	ID-(5)	.004,63	ID-(4)	.001,15
CC-(4)	.006,85	CC-(7)	.004,72	CC-(5a)	.000,92
Bicausal and Circular Chains	.006,85	Bicausal Chain-(8)	.006,61	Circular Chain-(7)	.001,06

Note: *ID-(5), for example, stands for the relation (5) in the ID-system in the preceding chapter, and the same logic is applied to all other notations. The demand relation of the circular chain and the price relation of the bicausal chain have no predictive powers due to the nature of the respective systems.*

equations (rather than by a model itself). These variables should account for unpredictable variables as invention and innovation, new legislation, war and crisis. To account for such events, some educated guesswork may be a better predictor than our formal approach. Thus serious doubt can be cast on rigorous comparison of ex-ante predictions for the conclusion of this study. For these reasons, a tentative ex-ante prediction is presented below solely for future reference rather than as a complement to compare the performance of the alternative systems.

Ex-post Prediction.—The measure of prediction accuracy for the observation range expressed by Theil's inequality coefficient is presented in the preceeding table.

Because Theil's is within the range of $0 \leq T \leq 1$ and $T = 0$ indicates perfect prediction, it is notable that all systems perform well regardless of their marginal accuracy differences. As the ID-protagonists claim their

ty Coefficient in light of the 'testability' of model stability; however, this selection is adopted to prevent any impression that our case study is biased in favor of the CC-system. See A. Gadd and H. Wold, "The Janus Quotient: A Measure for the Accuracy of Prediction," *Econometric Model Building*, ed. by H. Wold (Amsterdam: North-Holland Publishing Company, 1963), pp. 299–35.

predictions by reduced equations for the quantity demanded and supplied are slightly more accurate than those of the other systems. However, the price variable prediction is a little more accurate in the CC-system than the reduced price equation in the ID-system. This is an interesting result, because in some cases it is not true that the reduced equation of the ID-system is necessarily a better predictor of endogenous variables.

Ex-ante prediction.—The results from this study of 1950–1966 annual data are compared with the 1967 published actual values, except the inventory as shown in Table 1 of the preceding chapter. The following table shows their actual and predicted values in logarithms together with Theil's.

Table 4

Tin-Can Industry Case Study Results: Actual and Predicted Values in Logarithms Together with Theil's Inequality Coefficient

Actual Values	1. Equation Number 2. Predicted Values 3. (Theil's)			
	ID-System	CC-System	Bicausal Chain	Circular Chain
Demand:				
1.112,27	1. (5a):	(7)	(8)	
	2. 1.087,71	1.102,32	1.120,68	N.A.[3]
	3. (.011,16)	(.004,49)	(.003,77)	
Price:	1. (6)			(7a)
1.755,52	2. 1.756,29	N.A.[2]	N.A.[3]	1.757,29
	3. (.000,22)			(.000,51)
Supply:	1. (5)	(4)		
	2. 1.110,69	1.111,32	1.111,32	1.111,32
N.A.[1]	3. N.A.[4]	N.A.[4]	N.A.[4]	N.A.[4]

Notes: *N.A.*[1] *stands for no data available; N.A.*[2] *stands for not applicable for the system due to N.A.*[1]*; N.A.*[3] *stands for not applicable due to the nature of the system; and N.A.*[4] *stands for not applicable due to N.A.*[1]. *Other notational meanings remain the same as in Table 3 above.*

For the quantity demanded, the bicausal chain system performs relatively better than the CC-system which, in turn, performs better than the ID-system; for prices, the ID-system is a bit better than the circular chain system however it is not possible to judge the CC-system due to the non-availability of the finished inventory data for 1967.

Above all, the performance of all systems has proved to be more or less satisfactory in light of the simplicity of the models and the heavy constraint of building similar models. We are not disappointed in the results of only marginal superiority of the theoretically rigorous CC-system over the dilemma-inherent-ID-system in our tin-can case study. Regardless of the favorable treatment of the ID-system in the test-run, the marginal superiority of the CC-system remains significant due to the light it can shed on future empirical studies. Of course the case study is subject to challenge and it is willingly accepted that "one swallow cannot bring Spring." However, neither is it possible for several swallows and we must be content with the results of our case study at this moment. (This author plans further empirical studies of producers' goods on the market and economy-wide levels for econometric model-building by use of the CC-system.) Put another way, the demonstration of the theoretical superiority of the CC-system is more than satisfactory for this paper and the case study shall be validated when further empirical applicability of these theoretical arguments is established.

In closing this comparative study, we reiterate our deep confidence in Professor Wold's higher level of aspiration in dynamic econometric model-building with time series data and in the power of his path-breaking Proximity Theorem. With this consideration in mind, this study has functioned as an introductory exploration into the problem of ascertaining workable market models. Much study remains undone, and as a concluding point we offer the following conjecture and proposals for future investigation: (1) the Proximity Theorem justifies, *mutatis mutandis*, the triangular matrix in most econometric structural models; (2) assuming the above conjecture to be true, further generalization of the Proximity Theorem, as well as this author's corollaries to the theorem, must be developed and tested under real conditions—possibly for the skillful employment of instrumental variables and lagged variables to overcome some peculiar case and yield empirical results through time series analysis; (3) the most crucial and fundamental problem in econometric model-building is to produce an adequate specification of economic behavior relations, rather than only concentrating on estimation techniques to complement specification errors. Specifically, in market model-building, research emphais should be directed toward comprehending the nature of market economic-reasoning and data, prior to the testing for statistically appropriate estimation techniques.

BIBLIOGAPHY AND INDEX

BIBLIOGRAPHY

Books

Adams, Walter, ed. *The Structure of American Industry*. 3rd ed. New York: Macmillan Company, 1961.

Allen, R. G. D. *Mathematical Analysis for Economists*. New York: St. Martin's Press, 1967.

Ayer, Alfred J. *Language, Truth and Logic*. New York: Dover Publications, Inc., 1952.

Bain, Joe S. *Barriers to New Competition*. Cambrigde: Harvard University Press, 1956.

——. *Industrial Organization*. New York: John Wiley and Sons, Inc., 1959.

Blalock, Hubert M., Jr. *Causal Inferences in Nonexperimental Research*. Chapel Hill: University of North Carolina Press, 1964.

Burnstein, M. L. "The Demand for Household Refrigeration in the United States." *The Demand for Durable Goods*. Edited by Arnold C. Harberger. Chicago: University of Chicago Press, 1960.

Cournot, Augustin. *Researches into the Mathematical Principles of the Theory of Wealth*. Trans. by Nathaniel T. Bacon. New York: Macmillan Company, 1897.

Cramer, Harald. *Mathematical Methods of Statistics*. Princeton: Princeton University Press, 1946.

Christ, Carl F. *Econometric Models and Methods*. New York: John Wiley and Sons, Inc., 1966.

Duesenberry, J. S. *et al. The Brookings Quarterly Econometric Model of the United States*. Amsterdam: North-Holland Publishing Company, 1965.

Ellis, Howard S., ed. *The American Economic Association Readings in Business Cycle Theory*. Homewood, Ill.: Richard D. Irwin, 1944.

——. *A Survey of Contemporary Economics*. Philadelphia: Blakison, 1948.

Evans, G. C. *The Mathematical Introduction to Economics*. New York: McGraw-Hill, 1930.

Evans, Michael K. *Macroeconomic Activity: Theory, Forecasting, and Control: An Econometric Approach*. New York: Harper and Row Company, 1969.

Ezekiel, Mordecai and Karl A. Fox. *Methods of Correlation and Regression Analysis*. 3rd ed. New York: John Wiley and Sons, Inc., 1959.

Feigl, Herbert. "Note on Causality." *Readings on the Philosophy of Science*. Edited by Herbert Feigl and May Brodbeck. New York: Appleton-Century-Crofts, 1953.

Fisher, Franklin M. *A Priori Information and Time Series Analysis: Essays in Economic Theory and Measurement*. Amsterdam: North-Holland Publishing Company, 1962.

——. *The Identification Problem in Econometrics*. New York: McGraw-Hill Book Company, 1966.

Frisch, Ragnar. *Statistical Confluence Analysis by Means of Complete Regression Systems*. Oslo: University Institute of Economics, 1934.

Goldberger, Arthur S. *Econometric Theory*. New York: John Wiley and Sons, Inc., 1964.

——. *Topics in Regression Analysis*. New York: Macmillan Company, 1968.

Gordon, Robert Aaron and Lawrence R. Klein. *The American Economic Association Readings in Business Cycles*. Homewood, Ill.: Richard D. Irwin, 1965.

Grenander, Ulf, ed. *Probability and Statistics*. New York: John Wiley and Sons, Inc., 1959.

Hannan, E. J. *Time Series Analysis*. New York: John Wiley and Sons, Inc., 1960.

Hansen, Bent. *A Study in the Theory of Inflation*. London: George Allen and Unwin, Lts., 1951.

——. *The Economic Theory of Fiscal Policy*. Trans. by P. E. Burke. Cambridge: Harvard University Press, 1958.

Harberger, Arnold C., ed. *The Demand for Durable Goods*. Chicago: University of Chicago Press, 1960.

Hession, Charles H. "The Metal Container Industry." *The Structure of American Industry*. 3rd ed. Edited by Walter Adams. New York: Macmillan Company, 1961.

Hicks, John R. *Value and Capital*. 2nd ed. Oxford: The Clarendon Press, 1946.

Hildreth, C. and F. G. Jarrett. *Statistical Study of Livestock Production and Marketing*. Cowles Commission for Research in Economics, Monograph No. 15. New York: John Wiley and Sons, Inc., 1955.

Hood, William C. and Tjalling C. Koopmans, eds. *Studies in Econometric Method*. Cowles Commission for Research in Economics, Monograph 14. New York: John Wiley and Sons, Inc., 1953.

Houthakker, H. S. and Lester D. Taylor. *Consumer Demand in the United States, 1929–1970: Analysis and Projections*. Cambridge: Harvard University Press, 1966.

Hurwicz, Leonid. "Least Squares Bias in Time Series." *Statistical Inference in Dynamic Economic Models*, Edited by Tjalling C. Koopmans. New York: John Wiley and Sons, 1950.

——. "Generalization of the Concept of Identification." *Ibid.*

Jakacs, Lajos. *Stochastic Processes*. Trans. by P. Zador New York: John Wiley and Sons, Inc., 1960.

Johnston, J. *Econometric Methods.* New York: McGraw-Hill Book Company, 1963.

Klein, Lawrence R. *Economic Fluctuations in the United States, 1921–1941.* Cowles Commission for Research in Economics, Monograph No. 11. New York: John Wiley and Sons, Inc., 1950.

——. *A Textbook of Econometrics.* Evanston, Ill.: Row, Peterson, and Company, 1953.

——. *An Introduction to Econometrics.* Englewood Cliffs, N.J.: Prentice-Hall, Inc., 1962.

——. "Problems in the Estimation of Interdependent Systems." *Model Building in the Human Sciences.* Edited by Herman O. A. Wold. Monaco: Union Européenne D'Editions, 1966.

——, and Arthur S. Goldberger. *An Econometric Model of the United States, 1929–1952.* Amsterdam: North-Holland Publishing Company, 1955.

Kolmogorov. A. N. *Foundations of the Theory of Probability.* Trans. by Nathan Morrison, 2nd English ed. New York: Chelsea, 1950.

Koopmans, T. C., ed. *Statistical Inference in Dynamic Economic Models.* Cowles Commission for Research in Economics, Monograph 10. New York: John Wiley and Sons, Inc., 1950.

Leser, C. E. V. *Econometric Techniques and Problems.* Griffin's Statistical Monographs and Courses, No. 21. New York: Hafner Publishing Company, 1966.

Lindahl, Erik. *Studies in the Theory of Money and Capital.* London: Allen and Unwin, 1939.

Lundberg, Erik. *Studies in the Theory of Economic Expansion.* Stockholm, 1939, Reprints of Economic Classics. New York: Augustus M. Kelley, Bookseller, 1964.

Lyttkens, Ejnar. "Standard Errors of Regression Coefficients by Autocorrelated Residuals." *Econometric Model Building.* Edited by Herman Wold. Amsterdam: North-Holland Publishing Company, 1964.

Mckie, James A. *Tin Cans and Tin Plate: A Study of Competition in Two Related Markets.* Cambridge: Harvard University Press, 1959.

Main, O. W. *The Canadian Nickel Industry.* Toronto: University of Toronto Press, 1955.

Malinvaud, E. *Statistical Methods of Econometrics.* Chicago: Rand McNally and Company, 1966.

Marshall, Alfred. *Principles of Economics.* 8th ed. London: Macmillan Company, 1946.

Moore, Henry L. *Synthetic Economics.* New York: Macmillan Company, 1929.

Neyman, J., ed. *Proceedings of the Fourth Berkeley Symposium on Mathematical Statistics and Probability.* Vol. I. Berkeley: University of California Press, 1961.

Pontificiae Academiae Scientiarvm Scripta Varia. *Study Week on the Econometric Approach to Development Planning, October 7–13, 1963.* Amsterdam:

North-Holland Publishing Company, 1965.

Robinson, Enders. A "Structural Properties of Stationary Stochastic Processes with Application." *Brown University Symposium on Time Series Analysis.* Edited by M. Rosenblatts. New York: John Wiley and Sons, 1963.

——. "Wavelet Composition of Time-Series." *Econometric Model Building.* Edited by Herman Wold. Amsterdam: North-Holland Publishing Company, 1964.

Rosenblatt, M., ed. *Brown University Symposium on Time Series Analysis.* New York: John Wiley and Sons, 1963.

Russel, Bertrand. "On the Notion of Cause, with Application to the Free-Will Problems." *Readings in the Philosophy of Science.* Edited by Herbert Feigl and May Brodbeck. New York: Appleton-Century-Crofts, 1953.

Samuelson, Paul A. *Foundations of Economic Analysis.* Cambridge: Harvard University Press, 1947.

——. "Dynamic Process Analysis." *A Survey of Contemporary Economics.* Edited by H. S. Ellis, Philadelphia: Blakison, 1948.

Schultz, Henry. *The Theory and Measurement of Demand.* Chicago: University of Chicago Press, 1938.

Schwartz, Bernard. *The Supreme Court: Constitutional Revolution in Retrospect.* New York: Ronald Press, 1957.

Simon, Herbert A. "Causal Ordering and Identifiability." *Studies in Econometric Method.* Edited by William C. Hood and Tjalling C. Koopmans. New York: John Wiley and Sons, 1953.

Stocking, George W., ed. *Workable Competition and Antitrust Policy.* Nashville, Tenn.: Vanderbilt University Press, 1961.

Theil, Henri. *Economic Forecasts and Policy.* 2nd rev. ed. Amsterdam: North-Holland Publishing Company, 1961.

Tinbergen, Jan. *Statistical Testing of Business-Cycle Theories II: Business Cycles in the United States of America, 1919–1932.* Geneva: League of Nations, 1939.

——. *Econometrics.* Trans. by H. Rijken van Olst. Philadelphia: Blakiston, 1951.

Wold, Herman Ole Andreas. *A Study in the Analysis of Stationary Time Series.* 2nd ed. Appendix by Peter Whittle. Stockholm: Almqvist and Wiksell, 1954.

——, ed. *Econometric Model Building: Essays on the Causal Chain Approach.* Amsterdam: North-Holland Publishing Company, 1964.

——, scientific organizer. *Model Building in the Human Sciences.* Entretians De Monoco En Sciences Humaines Session 1964. Monaco: Union Européenne D'Editions, 1966.

——. "Ends and Means in Econometric Model Building: Basic Considerations Reviewed." *Probability and Statistics.* Edited by Ulf Grenander. New York: John Wiley and Sons, 1959.

——. "Unbiased Predictors." *Proceedings of the Fourth Berkeley Symposium on Mathematical Statistics and Probability*, Vol. I. Edited by J. Neyman. Berkeley: University of California Press, 1961.

——. "The Approach of Model Building: Crossroads of Probability Theory, Statistics and Theory of Knowledge." *Model Building in the Human Sciences.* Edited by Herman O. A. Wold. Monaco: Union Européenne D'Editions, 1966.

——. "Forecasting by Chain Principle." *Econometric Model-Building: Essays on the Causal Chain Approach.* Edited by Herman O. A. Wold. Amsterdam: North-Holland Publishing Company, 1964.

——. "A Graphic Introduction to Stochastic Processes." *Bibliography on Time Series and Stochastic Processes.* An International Team Project. Edited by Herman O. A. Wold. Cambridge: M.I.T. Press, 1965.

——, and Enders A. Robinson. "Minimum-Delay Structure of Least-Squares and *Eo-Ipso* Predicting Systems for Stationary Stochastic Processes." *Brown University Symposium on Time Series Analysis.* Edited by M. Rosenblatt. New York: John Wiley and Sons, Inc., 1963.

——, and Lars Juréen. *Demand Analysis: A Study in Econometrics.* New York: John Wiley and Sons, Inc., 1953.

Zellner, Arnold, ed. *Readings in Economic Statistics and Econometrics.* Boston: Little, Brown and Company, 1968.

Zeuthen, F. *Economic Theory and Method.* Cambridge: Harvard University Press, 1955.

Articles

Basmann, R. L. "A Generalized Classical Method of Linear Estimation of Coefficients in a Structural Equation." *Econometrica*, XXV (January, 1958), 1–12.

Bentzel, R. and H. Wold. "On Statistical Demand Analysis From the Viewpoint of Simultaneous Equations," *Skandinavisk Aktuarietidskrift*, XXIX (1946), 95–114.

——, and B. Hansen. "On Recursiveness and Interdependency in Economic Models." *Review of Economic Studies*, XXII (1945–1946), 153–68.

Cochrane, D. and G. H. Orcutt. "Application of Least-Squares Regressions to Relationships Containing Autocorrelated Error Terms." *Journal of the American Statistical Association*, XLIV (March, 1949), 32–61.

Dickson, Harold. "Logical Aspects of Identities in Mathematics and in Economics." *Kyklos*, XIII (1960), 261–72.

Durbin, J. "Estimation of Parameters in Time-Series Regression Models." *Journal of the Royal Statistical Society* (series B), XXII (January, 1960), 139–53.

——, and G. S. Watson. "Testing for Serial Correlation in Least Squares Regression, Part I and II." *Biometrika* (December 1950 and June 1951), 409–28 and 159–178.

Ezekiel, Mordecai. "The Cobweb Theorem." *Quarterly Journal of Economics*, LII (February, 1938), 255–80.

Fisher, Franklin M. "Generalization of the Rank and Order Conditions for Identifiability." *Econometrica*, XXVII (July, 1959), 431–47.

——. "On the Cost of Approximate Specification in Simultaneous Equation Estimation." *Econometrica*, XXIX (April, 1961), 139–70.

Fox, Karl A. "Structural Analysis and the Measurement of Demand for Farm Products." *Review of Economics and Statistics*, XXXVII (February, 1954), 57–66.

Frisch, Ragnar and Trygve Haavelmo. "The Demand for Milk in Norway." *Statsøkonomisk Tidsskrift*, LII (1938), 1–62.

Girshick, M. A. and Trygve Haavelmo. "Statistical Analysis of the Demand for Food: Examples of Simultaneous Estimation of Structural Equations." *Econometrica*, XV (April, 1947), 79–110.

Griliches, Ziv. "A Note on Serial Correlation Bias in Estimates of Distributed Lags." *Econometrica*, XXIX (January, 1961), 65–73.

Haavelmo, Trygve. "The Statistical Implications of a System of Simultaneous Equations." *Econometrica*, XI (January, 1943), 1–12.

——. "The Probability Approach in Econometrics." *Econometrica*, XII, Supplement (July, 1944), 1–118.

——. "The Role of the Econometrician in the Advancement of Economic Theory." *Econometrica*, XXVI (July, 1958), 1–12.

Kapp, William. "In Defense of Institutional Economics." *Swedish Journal of Economics*, LXX (March, 1968), 1–18.

Klappholz, K. and E. J. Mishan. "Identities in Economic Models." *Economica*, XXIX (May, 1962), 117–28.

Klein, Lawrence R. "Single Equation vs. Equation System Methods of Estimation in Econometrics." *Econometrica*, XXVIII (October, 1960), 866–71.

Koopmans, T. C. "Identification Problems in Economic Model Construction." *Econometrica*, XVII (April, 1949), 125–44.

Liu, T-Chung. "A Simple Forecasting Model for the U.S. Economy." *International Monetary Fund: Staff Paper*, IV (August, 1955), 434–66.

——. "Underidentification, Structural Estimation, and Forecasting." *Econometrica*, XXVIII (October, 1960), 855–65.

Mann, H. Michael. "Seller Concentration, Barriers to Entry, and Rates of Return in Thirty Industries, 1950–1960." *Review of Economics and Statistics*, XLVIII (August, 1966), 296–307.

Moore, Henry L. "Empirical Laws of Demand and Supply and the Flexibility of Prices." *Political Science Quarterly*, XXXIV (December, 1919), 546–67.

——. "A Moving Equilibrium of Demand and Supply." *Quarterly Journal of Economics*, XXXIX (May, 1925), 357–71.

Nerlove, Marc and Kenneth F. Wallis, "Use of the Durbin-Watson Statistics in Inappropriate Situation." *Econometrica*, XXXIV (January, 1966), 365–72.

Ohlin, Bertil. "Some Notes on the Stockholm Theory of Savings and Investment." *Economic Journal*, XLVII (Part I, March, 1937), 53–69 and (Part

II, March, 1937), 221–40.

Orcutt, G. "A Study of the Autoregressive Nature of the Time Series Used for Tinbergen's Model of the Economic System of the United States, 1919–1932." *Journal of the Royal Statistical Society*, CXI (1948), Series B, 1–53.

——, and D. Cochrane. "A Sampling Study of the Merits of Autoregressive and Reduced Form Transformations in Regression Analysis." *Journal of the American Statistical Association*, XLIV (September, 1949), 356–72.

Rao, Potluri and Zvi Griliches. "Small-sample Properties of Several Two-Stage Regression Methods in the Context of Auto-correlated Errors." *Journal of the American Statistical Association*, LXIV (March, 1969), 253–72.

Robinson, Joan."'The Choice of Model' at the Royal Statistical Society Seminar on 'the Present Position of Econometrics'." *Journal of the Royal Statistical Society*, Series A, Part III (1960), 274–8.

Simon, Herbert A. "Theories of Decision-Making in Economics and Behavioral Science." *American Economic Review*, XLIX (June, 1959), 253–83.

Strotz, Robert H. and H. O. A. Wold. "Recursive vs. Nonrecursive Systems: An Attempt at Synthesis: A Triptych on Causal Chain Systems," Part I. *Econometrica*, XXVIII (April, 1960), 417–27.

——. "Interdependence as a Specification Error: A Triptych on Causal Chain Systems," Part II. *Econometrica*, XXVIII (April, 1960), 428–42.

Taylor, Lester D. and Thomas A. Wilson. "Three-Pass Least Squares: A Method for Estimating Models with a Lagged Dependent Variable." *Review of Economics and Statistics*, XLVI (November, 1964), 329–46.

Theil, H. and A. L. Nagar. "Testing the Independence of Regression Disturbances." *Journal of the American Statistical Association*, LVI (December, 1961), 793–806.

Tinbergen, Jan. "Econometric Business Cycle Research." *Review of Economic Studies*, VII (1940), 61–86.

Wold, Herman Ole Andreas. "A Synthesis of Pure Demand Analysis," Parts I-III. *Skandinavisk Aktuarietidskrift*, XXVI (1943), 85–118 and 220–263; XXVII (1944), 69–120.

——. "A Theorem on Regression Coefficients Obtained From Successively Extended Sets of Variables." *Skandinavisk Aktuarietidskrift*, XXVIII (1945), 181–200.

——. "On Prediction in Stationary Time Series." *Annals of Mathematical Statistics*, XIX (1948), 558–67.

——. "Statistical Estimation of Economic Relationships." In *Proceedings of the International Statistical Conference*, V (1947). Reprinted as Supplement to *Econometrica*, XVII (July, 1949), 1–22.

——. "On Least-Square Regression with Autocorrelated Variables and Residuals." *Bulletin de l'Institut International Statistique*, XXXII (1950, 290–4.

——. "Dynamic Systems of the Recursive Type: Economic and Statistical Aspects." *Sankhya*, XI (1951), 205–16.

——. "Book Review." Review of *Statistical Inference in Dynamic Economic*

Models, by Tjalling C. Koopmans, ed. *Econometrica*, XIX (October, 1951), 474–7.

——. "Causality and Econometrics." *Econometrica*, XXII (April, 1954), 162–77.

——. "Causal Inference From Observational Data: A Review of Ends and Means." *Journal of the Royal Statistical Society*, Series A, Part I (1956), 28–61.

——. "Book Review." Review of *Statistical Study of Livestock Production and Marketing*, by C. Hildreth and F. G. Jarrett. *Kyklos*, IX (1956), 264–6.

——. "A Generalization of Causal Chain Models." *Econometrica*, XXVIII (April, 1960), 443–63.

——. "Construction Principles of Simultaneous Equations Models in Econometrics." *Bulletin de l'Institut International de Statistique*, XXVIII, No. 4 (1961), 111–36.

——. "On the Consistency of Least-Squares Regression." *Sankhya*, Serise A, XXV (1963), 211–15.

——. "A Letter Report to Professor P. C. Mahalanobis." *Sankhya*, Series A, XXV (1963), 309–20.

——. "Book Review." Review of *Causal Inferences in Nonexperimental Research*, by Hubert M. Blalock, Jr. *Econometrica*, XXXV (October, 1965), 879–80.

——. "A Fix-Point Theorem with Econometric Background: Part I, Theorem; Part II, Illustrations. Further Developments." *Arkiv För Matematik*, Band 6 nr 12 and nr 13 (1967), 209–220 and 221–240.

——, and Peter Faxer. "On the Specification Error in Regression Analysis." *Annals of Mathematical Statistics*, XXVIII (March, 1957), 265–67.

Working, Elmer J. "What Do Statistical 'Demand Curves' Show?" *Quarterly Journal of Economics*, XLI (February, 1927), 212–35.

Yule, G. U. "On a Method of Investigation Periodicities in Distributed Series, With Special Reference to Wolfer's Sunspot Numbers." *Philosophical Transactions, Royal Society*, CCXXVI (March, 1927), 265–67.

Zellner, Arnold. "Econometric Estimation with Temporally Dependent Disturbance Terms." *International Economic Review*, II (May, 1961), 164–78.

Documents

Bruce's Juices, Inc. v. American Can Company. 87 F. Supp 985 (1949).

Metal Statistics. New York: American Metal Market, up to 1968 edition.

Moody's Industrial Manuals. New York: Dun and Bradstreet, annual issues.

Russelville Canning Company v. American Can Company. 87 F. Supp 484 (1949).

U.S. Congress. Senate. Subcommittee on Antitrust and Monopoly. *Hearings: Economic Concentration*, Part I-IV. Washington, D.C.: Government

Printing Office, 1965.
U.S. Department of Agriculture. *Distributed Lags and Demand Analysis for Agricultural and Other Commodities.* U.S. Department of Agriculture Handbook No. 141. Washington, D.C.: Government Printing Office, 1958.
U.S. Department of Commerce Bureau of Census. *1963 Census of Manufactures.* MC 63(2)-34A. Washington, D.C.: Government Printing Office, 1966.
——. *Annual Survey of Manufactures.* Washington, D.C.: Government Printing Office, annual issues.
——. *1967 Census of Manufactures, Preliminary Report, General Statistics for Industry Groups and Industries.* MC 67 (P)-1. Washington, D.C.: Government Printing Office, April, 1969.
U.S. Department of Labor Bureau of Labor Statistics. *Wholesale Prices and Price Index.* Washington, D.C.: Government Printing Office, monthly issues.
U.S. v. Alcoa. 148 F. 2d. 416 (1945).
U.S. v. American Can Company. 87 F. Supp 18 (1949).
U.S. v. American Can Company. 230 F. Supp 859 (1916).
U.S. v. Continental Can Company, et al. 84 S. Ct. 1738, No. 369 (1964).
Wold, Herman Ole Andreas. *Bibliography on Time Series and Stochastic Processes.* An international team work. Cambridge: M,I.T. Press, 1965.

Unpublished Material

Schultz, Henry. "The Meaning of Statistical Demand Curves." Edited by E. Altschul. University of Chicago, February, 1930. (Mimeographed.)
Hession, Charles H. "Competition in the Metal Food Container Industry, 1916–1946." Unpublished Ph. D. dissertation, Columbia University, 1948.

INDEX